THE BREHON LAWS

A LEGAL HANDBOOK

BY

LAURENCE GINNELL

OF THE MIDDLE TEMPLE, BARRISTER-AT-LAW

D1572334

WHEN it became known some time ago that I had undertaken to lecture on the Brehon Laws before the Irish Literary Society, London, one friend congratulated me on the fine subject I had taken in hand, and another on the same day asked me why in the world had I chosen such an uninteresting subject. To these two friends, and the classes they typify, I respectfully dedicate this little volume.

L. G.

CONTENTS.

THE BREHON LAWS.

CHAPTER I.

ANCIENT LAW.

S in law and all other branches of learning some knowledge of one system is useful in the study of any other system, so also one cannot well appreciate the relative proportions and importance of what belongs to one nation without taking some account of the condition in the same respect at the same period of neighbouring nations with which a comparison may be instituted. For this reason I think our present subject should be introduced by a preliminary notice of the condition of

2

law in early times in neighbouring nations with which we are liable to be compared. We can, however, scarcely do more than glance at one such nation; and remembering where we are, and the circumstances of our country, the English nation seems the most appropriate for our purpose.

The first collection of Saxon laws into writing was made under Æthelbirht, king of Kent, after Saint Augustine had converted him to Christianity and baptised him. This occurred about the beginning of the seventh century, Saint Augustine having arrived in Kent in A.D. 597. Æthelbirht's was a collection of the most meagre scraps, such as only extreme poverty in this respect could make any people consider worth collecting or preserving. After that time collections of laws continued to be made occasionally in Kent and the various little kingdoms into which England was then divided; but none of them reached respectable dimensions until that of Alfred the Great, towards the end of the ninth century. Alfred is said to have been educated in Ireland. His is the earliest collection the English nation can show of any real value. Besides those given under Alfred's own name, it is probable that he may also be credited with the so-called Dooms of Ine.

It is believed that none of the originals of the early English laws, or works relating to law, were written in the language of the English people, that the originals in Saxon times were always in Latin, and those of Norman times in Latin or Norman-

French, and that the copies of the Saxon Dooms now extant are transcripts from the translations made for vulgar use. The originals of Acts of Parliament continued to be written in Norman-French down to the beginning of the sixteenth century, and the records in legal proceedings down to the middle of the eighteenth century. The brand of native inferiority, first impressed upon the people, continued thus long impressed upon the laws the people were bound to obey. Even in this year of grace, 1894, the royal assent is given to Acts of Parliament in words which neither the Queen nor her subjects understand, and which never were used by any generation of Englishmen.

Bearing in mind these few facts regarding the early condition and historical development of English law, we come in a proper mood to consider the most archaic system of law and jurisprudence of Western Europe, of which many records now exist, namely, what are now generally known as the Brehon Laws. This is not their real name. Irish Laws, or Gaelic Laws, would be a better name for English speakers to use ; but the thing meant has always been known to Gaelic speakers as Feineachus. A general term for all law, without special reference to that of Ireland, was Recht. But the law of the Gaels was Feineachus. It included Cāin Law, being that which was enacted or solemnly sanctioned by national assemblies, was of universal obligation, and could be administered only by professional judges ; and it also included Urradhus Law, which was law relating to local matters, modified by local assemblies and by local customs, and which might be administered by the Flaiths who were not professional lawyers.

Inquirers into the native antiquities of Western Europe naturally turn to Cæsar to learn what was the state of things he found existing in Gaul; and if that could be ascertained with certainty, we might reasonably assume that the state of things in Ireland at that and at a later period was not very different. But although it was very good of Cæsar to write so much as he did, his mind was far too much occupied with Cæsar to be troubled recording many facts relating to mere barbarous life, or with adequately checking those recorded. Cæsar and other Roman writers give it to be understood that the Gauls on some occasions sacrificed human beings to their gods; and some modern writers calmly assume, as a matter beyond question, that the Gauls "sacrificed human beings in hecatombs," and that the Druids presided over these horrible butcheries. The innate absurdity of such assumptions might have prevented their expression were it not that the ghastly and sensational grows upon and takes possession of the mind that conceives it, until from excessive fulness the temptation to communicate it becomes irresistible. When communicated, it strikes the hearer or reader more forcibly and effectually than truth, modest and sober, can ever hope to do. Remembering what gross and scandalous falsehoods are sometimes deliberately told of our own contemporaries, even by people of respectable and sanctimonious exterior, I cannot admit that there is any truth in those stories of the Gauls and their Druids who are unable to return with their explanation. It is probable that either Cæsar was misinformed or some ceremony, observed by the Gauls in putting criminals to death, was misinterpreted to him or by him. At all events, there is no reason at all to think that human sacrifice ever was practised in Ireland.

Owing to the isolated geographical position of Ireland, references to it by Roman and other ancient writers are comparatively few and of a vague and general character ; but fortunately a very full study of Gaelic Ireland can be made from native sources without consulting other authorities except for corroboration. Many leading facts of Irish history have been quite satisfactorily ascertained to the extent of three hundred years before Cæsar's time. It would, however, be difficult to lay down a connected and consequential narrative until about A.D. 250, in the reign of King Cormac. This was the time at which some of the laws we are about to consider were reduced to their present form, though they had existed in some other form long before. Those laws, as well as the laws comprised in the greater collection made two centuries later, had probably existed, as laws, a thousand years before Cormac's time. Almost all the Brehon Laws had actually reached their full proportions and maturity about the time that Alfred was re-

ducing to order the scraps of elementary law he
found existing amongst his people. It is with the
remains of the laws that then existed in Ireland—
boulders from the dun—that we are mainly concerned. Needless to say, they were not written
in a foreign tongue. No foreign mind conceived
them. No foreign hand enforced them. They
were made by those who, one would think, ought
to make them: the Irish. They were made for
the benefit of those for whose benefit they ought to
have been made: the Irish. Hence they were good;
if not perfect in the abstract, yet good in the sense
that they were obeyed and regarded as priceless
treasures, not submitted to as an irksome yoke.
And the presence or absence of popular sympathy
with law I take to be a true test of the quality of
that law and the very touchstone of good government. Originating in the customs of early settlers
in times beyond the reach of history, these laws
grew in volume and in perfection down to the time
mentioned; after which, though continually applied,
though copied, re-copied, and commented upon, little
of substantial value was added to them. They prevailed over the whole country until the arrival of
the Anglo-Normans, and they prevailed over the
whole country except the Pale until the beginning
of the seventeenth century. In such a great length
of time they must have undergone more or less
change; but the political condition of the country
during all that time being wholly adverse to true
development, the actual changes may be taken to

have been the very least possible. In proportion
as they lost in utility owing to this cause, they now
gain in value to us as archaic relics. And not
to us alone, but to continental peoples; to some
especially, because they claim a common origin with
with us and have little or no native records reaching
so far back as ours; to all, for their philological and
general antiquarian interest, and because in these
laws can be studied nearer to their source than
anywhere else the ancient legal ideas of a Celtic
people expanding free from external control. Other
Celtic nations were subjected to Roman sway and
modified by Roman influences, and now little can
be ascertained regarding their pre-Roman state
except through Roman sources. The isolated
position of our country, perhaps a disadvantage
on the whole, had, at all events, the effect of
leaving one nation truly Celtic, while its kindred
on the Continent were being transmuted. The
incursions of the Danes produced the first external
effect on our laws; but only to the extent of stopping
their growth and development and throwing what
may be called the organs of development into
disorder, from which, owing to historical causes,
they never recovered. The Danes never obtained
supreme control over Ireland, as they did over
England and the North of Gaul, but they harassed
and plundered the people, lowered the standard
of religion, morality, and patriotism, and fatally
smote the institutions of the country, so that from
the first arrival of the Danes in A.D. 795 the nation

and its laws ceased to progress. The laws were
petrified and fossilised, and remained at the ex-
pulsion of the Danes what they had been at their
arrival. And they remain practically the same
still; for to conquer the Danes at Clontarf, though
hard the task, was easier than to restore efficiency
and fresh growth to institutions once paralysed,
or to revive national patriotism, the stagnation of
which had become normal. Those institutions had
not recovered their former vigour when the Anglo-
Normans came, threw the country once more into
turmoil, and kept it so. The Normans, like the
Danes, had conquered England and established
their own institutions there; but even they never
conquered the whole of Ireland, and institutions
of their introduction flourished only in the Pale, a
small district whose extent varied with the fortunes
of war, rarely exceeding four of the present Leinster
counties. The Anglo-Norman settlers in other parts
of Ireland conformed in the main to the Irish laws,
with here and there some slight modifications which
were strictly transgressions. Successive English
Governments sent over Deputies and Governors,
nominally to rule Ireland, but really to rule the
Pale, to create as much dissension as possible
beyond that limit, and at any rate to maintain a
foothold. A country so circumstanced, partially
conquered, the mutilated prey for which two nations
hungered and tore and thwarted each other, was
one in which the rational development of law or
of anything else was scarcely possible. And thus

it comes to pass that the laws may be said to remain to-day substantially what they were before
the arrival of the Danes more than a thousand
years ago.

CHAPTER II.

THE EXISTING REMAINS OF IRISH LAW.

OST of the literary remains of ancient Ireland that are really valuable and characteristically beautiful appear to belong to the same distant period; and therefore they are highly interesting philologically, quite apart from the intrinsic beauty of some, which is very great. Of all those remains, those dealing with law are, considered as literature, the least attractive. But their value to the earnest student of antiquity is inferior to none, but is perhaps superior to all the rest, owing to their rigorously authentic character. The charge of having been produced or tinged by imagination cannot be made against the laws, rules, and customs which actually controlled the daily lives, conduct, and destinies of our ancestors, and under which they laboured, fought, played, and prayed, as occasion demanded. These remains at least represent what were once the realities of life ; and the knowledge and the study of them must, with absolute certainty, help so far as they go to dispel the mist of years. We are brought if possible still closer to the actuality of individual life by the suits and judgments which are scattered through these laws for the purpose of illustrating their principles and their application. And while one reads, if perchance his taste should be of wider scope, he is enabled to gather incidentally much archæological information not strictly legal, but of a kind difficult if at all possible to glean from other sources, all stamped here with the authenticity of the law, and not less valuable for being thus given without design.

The fact is as expressive as it is painful that, beyond the limited operations of one or two stunted societies, almost the whole of our Gaelic records, laws, and literature remained in manuscript, and practically inaccessible until the middle of the nineteenth century, and that much of those materials remain so even now at the close of the century. Most of those manuscript books, and some of the longer tracts, the legal as well as the others, refer to and quote from other and older books, sometimes by name, sometimes by a description which had become recognised as a name, as the White Book of such a person, the Black Book of such a place, the Yellow Book or the Speckled Book of So-and-so; and sometimes the reference is general, as to other versions or other books. From these references it is evident that, although we still possess a great deal of written matter as compared with other countries, far more than we possess has been lost. This is not wonderful in the circumstances of Ireland, but it is none the less matter for regret. Still, competent judges say that our extant manuscript materials are, both for antiquity and intrinsic worth, treasures such as no nation north of the Alps can boast of. Any one who suspects this for a Gaelic exaggeration had better visit the Royal Irish Academy and have his incredulity speedily and agreeably cured by the evidence of his own eyes. Whatever else may be said of those remote ancestors of ours, it must be admitted that they were singularly devoted to literature, and if the remains of their work have a high value and interest for strangers and Teutons, to us whose heritage they are, and whose privilege and pride it is to call Ireland our native land, they should be not alone valuable and interesting, but sacred. A people possessing such precious monuments and indifferent to them would certainly be unworthy of the race and country that produced them, and would merit the censure of civilised mankind. Do we value these treasures as we ought? Do we escape the censure or fall under it? Apparently we fall under it; and this while we possess the power, and at heart the desire, to escape it. In practice we neglect what in theory we venerate; and thus, as in other respects, we perpetuate against ourselves as a nation a wrong begun by others.

But this extraordinary condition of things has
not come about spontaneously, as a reader of Mr.
Standish O'Grady's *Heroic Period* might infer. Mr.
O'Grady, in common with all who study the subject,
laments the fact that Irishmen of the present day
devote so little attention to the extraordinary wealth
of historic treasures they possess. But the implied
assertion is only half a truth, and the candour that
prompts telling half a truth when bitter to Irishmen
will justify telling the remaining half though it
should be bitter to Englishmen ; in addition to
which we, as real inquirers, are entitled to the
whole truth. Ours is the bitterness of loss, theirs
the bitterness of guilt. If to be made wince be
a wholesome discipline for us, it cannot be unwhole-
some for our neighbours. Our alleged indifference,
then, so far as it exists, is neither native nor natural
to us, but is a plant of English culture and a necessary result of the species of English rule that Ireland
has experienced. Both Danes and Normans, the
former especially, destroyed our manuscripts in
the course of warlike operations; but to modern
Englishmen from Elizabeth's time downwards—
Ireland's darkest age—to men who came not frankly
to plunder as the Danes did, but to govern us
and set us a bright example, some of them with
Bibles in their hands and Scripture on their lips;
to these men the distinction is due of having, in
times of so-called peace and in cold blood, burned
and destroyed our books, hanged or hunted their
owners as vermin, made it criminal to teach or learn

the language in which they were written, or indeed to teach or learn at all;—the alternative or rather twofold object of this enlightened statesmanship being to drive the Celts out of their native land or reduce them to savagery in it. Both policies have had a large measure of success; neither has completely succeeded. The Irishmen who, when their own fortunes and hopes, like those of their country, were utterly ruined, risked liberty and life itself during that perilous age for the preservation of those precious monuments of the past, must be not charged with indifference, but credited with devotedness almost equalling that of the original writers. As few ancient nations have been more fruitful in original literary effort, so few modern nations have shown more attachment to literary treasures than the Irish; and in no other case that I am aware of has that natural and creditable attachment been subjected to such a terrible strain. On this very subject let me quote from Dr. Sullivan, the learned editor of O'Curry's *Lectures on the Manners and Customs of the Ancient Irish.* Dr. Sullivan says, "During the first part of the eighteenth century the possession of an Irish book made the owner a suspected person, and was often the cause of his ruin. In some parts of the country the tradition of the danger incurred by having Irish manuscripts lived down to within my own memory; and I have seen Irish manuscripts which had been buried until the writing had almost faded, and the margins rotted away, to avoid the danger their discovery would en-

tail at the visit of the local yeomanry." Was not
that a pretty state of things? What Dr. Sullivan
saw was of course but a single isolated instance
after the real danger had passed away; but from
it we may judge how much was destroyed under
Elizabeth, under Cromwell, under William the Third,
and throughout the whole of that dark age; and the
calculation is materially assisted by the lurid stories
heard by some of us at our fathers' firesides. It
is morally certain that at the present moment some
priceless Irish manuscripts are mouldering away in
old walls, caves, graves, and other places under the
earth. The causes of our apparent indifference to
historical treasures are so obvious that they cannot
possibly have escaped even the most casual and
careless reader of our modern history; into the
soul of every Irishman worthy of the name they
must be indelibly burnt. Every one who cares at
all about Ireland knows them, and knows that the
real wonder is that we have any such treasures
and that anybody cares for them. Mr. O'Grady
has an intimate knowledge of all this. Yet he
seizes an occasion to censure, neither Elizabeth nor
Cromwell, neither the imported yeomanry who were
planted on the fat lands of our people nor the
governors who planted them there, but Irishmen.
Here surely is perceptible the taint of that bitterly
anti-Irish institution, Trinity College, Dublin. A
man educated anywhere else in the world would,
in the premises, place the blame on other shoulders,
and if he blamed Irishmen at all in this connection

it would be on very different grounds. It does not afford much matter for pride on that side or for shame on this that the Irish people could be, and were, by brute force, robbed of their learning for the purpose of civilising them. But brute force has not yet robbed them of their intelligence or of their love of learning. These, though in a measure rendered latent, still exist and will yet respond to more rational treatment. The number of persons who can read the manuscripts has indeed been reduced ; but the number who would risk much in their preservation is as large as ever ; and certainly their veneration would not be less if the vellum were found to smell of turf-smoke contracted in the course of such a history. However this may be, and whatever may be thought of ourselves, we have at least this much matter for legitimate satisfaction that the existence of these manuscripts renders it impossible for any one with a decent regard for truth to charge our ancestors with ignorance. Commercially it were better for us if the order of merit were reversed ; but however low we may have fallen we have not reached the depth at which the commercial view alone is adopted. Neither man nor nation lives by bread alone, and if we are satisfied that merit rests where it does, no one else has a right to complain.

In spite of the burning and burying and drowning of manuscripts, a vast number still exist in public libraries and in private collections, in Ireland, in England, and on the Continent. Some of those relating to law are separate works, while others are written on the same vellum or otherwise bound up together with histories, genealogies, poems, religious works, and the like. All have come down by successive transcription. Of the more important works there are duplicate copies, hardly any of them being quite complete, and most of them differing slightly in text owing to the causes which similarly affect all ancient manuscripts, as want of time or want of diligence on the part of transcribers. Most of the existing legal manuscripts are believed to have been written—that is, copied from older ones —between the beginning of the twelfth and the end of the fourteenth century. None of the originals, which were written in the fifth century, now exist ; nor are the existing manuscripts thought to have been copied directly from those originals. They are considered to be copies of copies. Repeated transcripts had already been made with, on each occasion, some modernisation here and there of the antiquated phraseology, or with the introduction of a gloss or a commentary to render the matter intelligible. The laws were originally written in the Bearla Feini, the Fenian dialect of Gaelic. As this language in course of time tended to become obsolete the laws tended to become unintelligible, and the tenacious adherence to old forms of expression common to all laws had to be severed or counteracted in some way. The transcribers did not act according to any uniform plan, nor did any transcriber continue throughout the work the mode

3

of treatment with which he began, but each from
time to time translated early into late Gaelic to the
extent of some words that were in his time difficult,
or left the original phrase standing, and supplied a
gloss or a commentary. Each may be considered
to have done the best that his circumstances permitted, for writing was not a thousand years ago
the simple thing it now is. The great antiquity,
both of the original text and of the commentaries,
is shown in several ways. Quotations from both are
found in works admittedly written not later than the
tenth century. Some parts of these older commentaries, although written later than the text, are
still very ancient, and besides they contain, as
quotations or otherwise, some fragments of traditional law fully as archaic as any in the text. The
language being of a highly technical, elliptical and
abbreviated character too, and devoid of all proper
definitions, is now scarcely intelligible to speakers
of what is nominally the same language; and of
the few who can read still fewer can confidently
construe. Even some of the Gaelic transcribers of
the Middle Ages may possibly have erred in its
construction.

Imagine a work treated at one time in the manner
described, and then, after another century or two
had elapsed, treated again in a similarly irregular
fashion by another transcriber—here a literal copy,
there a translation, in another place a gloss or a
commentary, to keep pace with the further changes
in the spoken language, and you will have a fair

idea of the present condition of the Brehon Laws.
What are thus spoken of under the general name of
commentaries contain much matter not suggested
by that title.   Many independent decisions and dicta,
old and current, are inserted under particular texts
with which some of them have little or no connection, but as the most suitable or most convenient
place the writer could find for them.   The most
valuable of the commentaries were written before
the existing manuscripts were transcribed, and they
interpret not alone obscure passages in the text but
the substantive law itself.   Later commentaries
were written by various hands on the present manuscripts, and even these may not be all original.
They were written between the original lines, on
the margin, at the foot, wherever room was found.
For the most part a text is given; but in some
instances the whole of the original text does not
now exist, only the opening words of passages being
retained in the existing transcripts.   These opening
words, used as headings or catchwords, are quite
meaningless in themselves as they now stand; but
of course they were full of meaning for those whose
business it was to know what followed.   They are
now followed by commentaries from which may be
gathered the substance of the original, as a commentary on the Lord's Prayer might be headed with
the words "Our Father."   Comments upon law
and glosses upon words are inserted without any
apparent attempt to keep them separate, and with
the latter are frequently given an assortment of

etymological speculations in which the writers dis-
play some knowledge of what they call "the four
principal languages of the world," Hebrew, Greek,
Latin, and Gaelic.   Derivations of words, of rules,
and of customs are suggested almost at random,
and are no more reliable than similar attempts of
ancient Roman writers ; some of them being clearly
fabulous and not seriously meant.   When the commentary is mainly etymological and in the nature of
a translation of the text, and both are translated
into English side by side, the result in the English
is an unpleasant tautological repetition of the same
thing.   Sometimes the commentators purport to
explain the text, start with that apparent object but
with a relative pronoun for which it is now difficult
to find an antecedent, plunge *in medias res*, and end
by leaving the whole matter quite as obscure as
the text had left it.   Accounts of the effects of
particular judgments are also met with, some of
them legendary, others of real value.   According
to one commentator, "Sencha MacColl Cluin was
not wont to pass judgment until he had pondered
upon it in his breast the night before."   This
probably refers to a judgment in a grave case
involving human life.   Judges of the Hebrew nation
in early times were accustomed to fast the night
and morning before passing a death sentence.   The
text of the old laws is fairly self-consistent throughout.   The commentaries, as might be expected from
the manner in which they were written by different
hands at different times, are not always reconcil-

able, and there is a good deal of tiresome repetition in them. The translators have found them useful in many cases, misleading in some. They are interesting throughout.

The condition just described involves so many difficulties in dealing with these laws, that Gaelic scholars generally in the last century believed the translation of them to have become impossible, the key having been lost. If occasionally an educated Englishman of the present day finds the legal documents in which he is personally concerned hard to understand, though assisted by his knowledge of the actual facts to which they relate, his knowledge of the language and of contemporary life in all its phases, how much more difficult must it not be to draw legal writings of a distant past from their dust and cobwebs and the greater load of impedimenta just mentioned, to understand them fully and to render them correctly, when the system of life which those laws contemplated and provided for has vanished from the earth leaving no derivative institutions in existence ?

In 1852 a Royal Commission was appointed to translate and publish the *Ancient Laws and Institutes of Ireland,* and thus bring them within the reach of English readers. The nature of the undertaking may be judged from the difficulties enumerated, and many others must have been encountered in the actual performance of the work. It is only just that we who can now read those laws at our ease should remember those difficulties and be grateful to the

learned men who have surmounted them; and we
cannot be surprised to find that, distinguished
scholars though they were and are, they have
actually failed to understand some passages which
they have translated; and they repeatedly empha-
sise the fact that their translation is in certain parts
conjectural only and must not be taken as final or
satisfactory.   Many technical terms relating to
status, ranks and degrees, as well as names of fines,
diseases of horses, &c., are retained in the English
untranslated; some because the translators were
unable to satisfy themselves as to the true meaning;
others because the words have no direct or adequate
equivalents in English, and would demand a tedious
circumlocution each time they had to be used; others
because, although the translators understood them,
and could find suitable equivalents in English, yet
remembering that the ancient Irish manuscript
materials have never in modern times been fully
investigated, the translators have, with commend-
able modesty and patriotism, retained the original
words, appending to them temporary explanations
to serve until that better time comes for which, without being politicians, we are all permitted to hope,
when those laws can be thoroughly analyzed and
explained.   This latter work is one of greater
difficulty still, and should be undertaken only by
men free from the preliminary work of translating,
free from the necessity of making a living, and
endowed with a keen and unconquerable genius for
minute research.   This was not the work under-

taken by the Commissioners; it still awaits the enthusiast.

That these laws should be found difficult is not wonderful, seeing that the English are now unable to translate some technical terms in the Saxon laws so late as those of the reign of Cnut.

The Brehon Law Commissioners have already published, at different dates as the work proceeded, four volumes of the *Ancient Laws of Ireland*, and a fifth is now (1894) in the press. The ancient law book called the Senchus Mōr, or rather all that remains of it, was the first selected for publication, as being one of the oldest and most important portions of the Brehon Laws which have escaped destruction. This ancient work occupies the whole of the first volume of the translations, the whole of the second volume, except an appendix of scraps, and a portion of the third volume. The part of the Senchus Mōr given in the first volume deals directly with the law of distress, that is the seizure by distraint of property for the satisfaction of debt, and only incidentally with other subjects. It will be seen in the chapter on distress why this branch of law required so much space and was given this extraordinary prominence. This first volume of the translations was published in 1865. The second volume, which was published in 1869, contains very interesting fac-similes of ancient writing, and more than four hundred pages of text of the Senchus Mōr, consisting of the completion of the law of distress, the law of services of hostage sureties (from which I

have not drawn for the present occasion), the law of
fosterage, the law of tenure, and the law of social
connections, all of which are of the highest interest.
The text of this volume is preceded by a long
dissertation, the object of which is to prove that
Saint Patrick was a Briton. Interesting though
this might be as a separate publication, dependent
for its worth solely on its author's name, I cannot
but think it out of place here where the question
cannot be discussed on equal terms. In the third
volume of the translations, published in 1873, further
specimens of ancient writing are given. The volume
contains a long general preface, followed by a special
introduction to the remaining portion of the Senchus
Mōr—the Corus Bescna—which itself occupies
seventy-nine pages. This is the conclusion of the
Senchus Mōr so far as it is now known to exist.
The Corus Bescna, or customary law, is said to have
been the fifth book of the original work, there being
then more than five books. Possibly the remaining
portions exist somewhere, but they have not been
discovered. The Senchus Mōr, as now given to us,
is not clearly divided into books. Portions of the
original work having been lost, we may be thankful
to get the remainder kept together in any way.
After the conclusion of the Senchus Mōr in the third
volume, we are given nearly one hundred pages of
preface to the Book of Aicill, followed by the Book of
Aicill itself, which, with an appendix, occupies over
five hundred pages. The fourth volume opens with
a long and elaborate introduction containing a dis-

cussion of the different subjects treated in the volume, but dealing especially with the Irish family and clan system. The text of this volume consists of a number of tracts selected as especially illustrating the land laws of the ancient Irish, the law of taking possession, and the laws affecting the constitution of *clan* and *fine* and the rights and obligations of members of those two organisations. I have no knowledge of the contents of the fifth volume now in type.

CHAPTER III.

THE SENCHUS MŌR.

ROM the synopsis just given of the work already done by the Brehon Law Commission, it will be seen that the Senchus Mōr, or Grand Old Law, occupies the first and largest part of it. That ancient work was designed to be a comprehensive and more or less codified embodiment of the laws which were of universal obligation over the whole country before the arrival of St. Patrick. Outside it such special rules as occasion demanded were made or sanctioned by local assemblies, but all were so framed as to harmonise with and be subject to the general law as set forth in the Senchus Mōr. This is a great collection, not of statutes, proclamations, or commands of any sort, but of laws already known and observed from time immemorial; call

them rules or customs if you will, but having the
force of laws, authoritatively set forth in this work,
partly by way of direct statements or propositions,
partly by way of judicial decisions in actual cases.
The work contains nothing of the harsh, peremptory,
imperative style of early Roman law. The writers
do not say, Go, do this, or Go, do that, or If a man
does so and so, let him be hurled from the Tarpeian
Rock. No; they do not enact anything. Pursuing
the more gentle course of the later Roman lawyers,
they state what the law is, support the statement
with the decisions of the wisest Brehons, and then
leave the law to prevail *suo vigore*. They explain
that the men of Erinn having considered the matter
in times past decided that it was best it should be
so, and that nobles, chiefs and tribes have loyally
observed these laws. Any alteration really desired
could be effected, according to its scope, either in the
local assembly or in the national assembly. Being
Plebiscita in the very best sense, not emanating from,
the mouth of a tyrant but from the wisest heads of
the nation, it followed as a natural consequence that
these laws were obeyed and venerated as the spirit
by which the nation ought to be ruled. There was
therefore no occasion for the imperative, none for
coercion. It was needless to force people to do that
which they took pride in doing. Besides, the laws
having been made by the nation itself were, of course,
designed to promote and secure its wellbeing and
happiness, and were therefore broadly just and
generally found favourable to every good purpose.

One of the Gaelic commentators says of the
contents of the Senchus Mōr, " In the Senchus Mōr
were promulgated the four laws, namely—(1) the
law of fosterage ; (2) the law relating to free tenants
and the law relating to base tenants ; (3) the law of
social relationship ; (4) the binding of all by their
verbal contracts ; for the world would be in a state
of confusion if verbal contracts were not binding."
This is a very inadequate presentation of the contents of the work.   The most important branch of
law dealt with in the work is wholly omitted from
this enumeration, and those mentioned are given
neither in the order of their arrangement nor in that
of their importance.   But the commentary goes on :
" The binding of all to their good and bad contracts
prevents the lawlessness of the world.   Except the
five contracts which are dissolved by the Feini,
even though they be perfected—(1) The contract
of a labourer without his chief ; (2) the contract of
a monk without his abbot ; (3) the contract of the
son of a living father without the father ; (4) the
contract of a fool or mad woman ; (5) the contract
of a woman without her husband."   " In it was
established the *dire*-fine of each one according to his
dignity ; for the world was at an equality until the
Senchus Mōr was established."   These few quotations give an idea of the nature of the commentaries
and of the scope of the Senchus Mōr proper.

The Senchus Mōr was, according to the introduction to it, compiled at the suggestion and under
the supervision of St. Patrick in the time of King

Laeghaire (Leary), when Theodosius was Ard-Rīg of the world. The same introduction places St. Patrick's arrival in the ninth year of the reign of Theodosius as Ard-Rīg of the world, and in the fourth year of the reign of Laeghaire as Ard-Rīg of Erinn. Theodosius the Second is the emperor meant. While a mere child he succeeded his father Arcadius as Emperor of the East in A.D. 407. On the death of his uncle Honorius in 423, he became Emperor of the West also, and thus Ard-Rīg or monarch of the world. Nine years after this date was 432, which is also the date of the arrival of St. Patrick according to the Four Masters and other Irish authorities. Theodosius did not continue Emperor of the West during those nine years, but voluntarily resigned that position to Valentinian the Third and confined himself to the East again. However, as the East and West were long ruled as two parts of one empire rather than as two distinct empires, the same laws being promulgated simultaneously in both, the partial and friendly abdication of Theodosius may well have escaped the notice or comprehension of Irishmen in those times. In the commentary it is stated that at the end of nine years after the arrival of St. Patrick the Senchus Mōr was completed. That would be A.D. 441. In the *Annals of the Four Masters* it is said, " The age of Christ 438. The tenth year of Laeghaire. The Senchus Mōr and Feineachus of Ireland were purified and written." The work must have extended over several years, and those from 438 to 441 appear the most probable.

The laws, being wholly the production of pagans, needed some modification to reconcile them with the requirements of Christianity. St. Patrick having during seven or eight years of missionary work all over the country, as well as in the previous years of his bondage, learned in what respects the laws conflicted with his teaching and thwarted his efforts, desired, as well for the material welfare of the people as for the success of his mission, to have the laws amended. The most permanently and universally effective way in which this could be done was to have a simultaneous collection and revision of the laws decreed by a great assembly of the nation, and then to take care that the work should be actually performed by men imbued with the Christian spirit. Accordingly, " He requested the men of Erinn to come to one place to hold a conference with him. When they came to the conference the Gospel of Christ was preached to them all. . . . And when they saw Laeghaire and his druids overcome by the great science and miracles wrought in the presence of the men of Erinn, they bowed down in obedience to the will of God and Patrick, in the presence of every chief in Erinn. It was then that Dubhthach (pronounced *Dhoovah*) was ordered to exhibit the judgments and all the poetry (literature) of Erinn, and every law which prevailed amongst the men of Erinn, through the law of nature, and the law of seers, and in the judgments of the island of Erinn, and in the poets. Now the judgments of true nature which the Holy

Spirit had spoken through the mouths of the brehons and just poets of the men of Erinn from the first occupation of the island down to the reception of the faith were all exhibited by Dubhthach to Patrick. What did not clash with the Word of God in the written law and in the New Testament, and with the consciences of believers, was confirmed in the laws of the brehons by the ecclesiastics and the chief men of Erinn; for the law of nature was quite right, except the faith and its obligations, and the harmony of the Church and the people. And this is the Senchus Mōr." Yes, such is the Senchus Mōr, a name which it is said to have received not from the magnitude of the work but from the greatness of the number and nobility of the assembly by which it was sanctioned. This latter statement, however, is rendered doubtful by the existence of a Senchus Beg. (*Mōr*=Great. *Beg*=Little. *Senchus* is pronounced nearly *Shankus*).

It will be observed that the account just quoted treats the laws in the plainest possible terms as pre-existing, and neither as freshly enacted nor as imported. In another place the introduction is equally explicit on this point. Some of the commentaries written centuries later, when Christian zeal was greater than critical acumen or historical accuracy, attributed the origin of the laws to the influence of Cai, an imagined contemporary of Moses, who had learned the law of Moses before coming from the East. Of course this myth deserves no consideration. Cai is only another word for ollamh, or sage.

In other late commentaries, and also in other
writings in which reference is made to the laws,
so much importance is, by a pious exaggeration,
attached to what Saint Patrick had done that the
Senchus Mōr itself is called the *Cāin Phadraig*, or
Patrick's law. The abandonment of paganism may
have caused the discontinuance of some particular
species of actions, and hence some omissions from
the statement of the laws; the introduction and
enthusiastic adoption of Christianity profoundly
affected the moral and religious life of the people,
producing eventually new causes and new law; some
rules of Canon Law, or rather Church Law, introduced for ecclesiastical purposes, were quite novel
and therefore striking, and the Christian spirit
breathed through the whole law was important;
but the actual changes were few, and substantially
the laws remained the same as they had existed for
centuries before.

The number of the authors of the Senchus Mōr is
preserved in one of the alternative names given to it
in the introduction and in some of the commentaries.
In the introduction it is said, "*Nofis* therefore is
the name of the book, that is the knowledge of nine
persons." And again it says, "Nine persons were
appointed to arrange this book, namely, Patrick and
Benen and Cairnech, three bishops; Laeghaire and
Corc and Daire, three kings; Rossa mac Trechim,
a Doctor of Bearla Feini, Dubhthach, a Doctor of
Bearla Feini and a Poet, and Fergus the Poet."
Benen, Latinised Benignus, was Saint Patrick's

favourite disciple, and afterwards became a bishop
and a saint. He was a Munsterman by birth, but
was residing at Duleek at the time of Saint Patrick's
arrival. Cairnech, who is said to have been a native
of Cornwall, was also a follower of Saint Patrick.
He, too, became a bishop and a saint, and is
honoured as such in both the Irish and the English
calendars. Laeghaire, as already stated, was ard-
rīg at Tara, and was a son of Niall the Great, known
also as Niall of the Nine Hostages, who in his time
had overrun Britain and Gaul in much the same
fashion as the Danes of a later period overran those
countries. It is believed that Laeghaire did not
become a Christian. If he remained an infidel he
must have been a very tolerant one, for the principal
officers of his court appear to have become Christian
like the rest of the nation; he gave his sanction to
the convening of the assembly which ordered the
preparation of the Senchus Mōr, every facility for
carrying out the work, and in no way opposed the
modifications suggested by Saint Patrick; nor does
he appear to have raised any obstacle to the propa-
gation of Christianity. He died at Tara, and was
buried in one of the mounds there, standing and fully
armed, facing the south. Corc was the King of
Munster and resided at Cashel. He also is said
to have remained a pagan. He died in battle.
Daire was the sub-king of a portion of Ulster, and
chiefly from the fact that he afterwards gave the site
of Armagh to Saint Patrick to found his see, it is
inferred that he must have become a Christian.

4

Of the nine nominal authors, the remaining three were the learned men who really did the work. They were men specially qualified from the legal and national point of view, all three being eminent in all the learning of the time; and specially qualified from Saint Patrick's particular point of view, all being converts to Christianity. For Saint Patrick's missionary method was first to make a bold attempt to convert the learned and powerful. Besides their personal qualifications, those three men being specially chosen on this solemn occasion for the performance of a task of the greatest national importance, they were assiduously provided with whatever manuscript or other material of the kind existed, and given every possible assistance in the performance of the undertaking. Dubhthach mac ua Lugair was at once the chief brehon and chief bard of the nation, a position to be reached only by means of the highest legal and literary attainments. He was a man celebrated for centuries after, on what grounds scholars still have some means of judging, for several fragments of his poetry are still extant, in the libraries of the Royal Irish Academy and Trinity College, and in some libraries on the Continent. A later Gaelic commentator on the Senchus Mōr says, " Dubhthach mac ua Lugair put a thread of poetry around it for Patrick."

It was usual to state in ancient Irish manuscript books the Name of the Author, the Time of writing, the Place of writing, and the Occasion, Cause, or Object of writing. It was in accordance with this custom that the introduction to the Senchus Mōr gave the information just noticed; and it goes on to tell in the following words where the compilers sojourned at the different seasons of the year while the work proceeded : — " The place of the Senchus Mōr was Temhair in the summer and in the autumn, on account of its cleanness and pleasantness during those seasons ; and Rath-guthaird, where the stone of Saint Patrick is at this day in Glenn-na-Mbodhur, near Nith nemonnach, was the place during the winter and spring, on account of the nearness of its firewood and its water, and on account of its warmth in the time of winter's cold." Temhair, genitive Teamhrac, pronounced Tara, is now so called [Gaelic words are frequently adapted to English in the genitive, speakers of modern English being generally ignorant of true declension]. Glennavohur has been satisfactorily identified as a lovely sheltered glen near Nobber, in Meath. A small stream called the Nith flows through it, and in this stream still stands the stone called Saint Patrick's stone.

The manuscripts of the Senchus Mōr now existing are four in number :—

1. A comparatively full copy among the manuscripts of Trinity College, Dublin.

2. An extensive fragment in the British Museum.

3. A large fragment in Trinity College, Dublin.

4. Another large fragment in Trinity College, Dublin.

All these manuscripts were translated by Dr.

O'Donovan, and afterwards collated in consultation
with O'Curry and other Gaelic scholars, breaks and
obscure passages in one being made up and illus-
trated respectively from the others, and everything
done to render the translation as perfect as possible.

No credit whatsoever is due to Trinity College as
an institution for the preservation of the legal or
other ancient documents now stored there. When
it was dangerous to preserve them, they were preserved by Irish peasants in spite of the danger, in
spite of the system of government which created the
danger and of which Trinity College was a part and
an instrument ; and it was only when Ireland's
darkest age, which Trinity College had heralded,
was coming to an end, that most of those ancient
documents reached their present resting-place.

Some English critics have raised various objections against the possibility of the Senchus Mōr
having been compiled under the supervision of Saint
Patrick, as, for instance, that he had enough to do
besides, that he could not have been a member of
the Irish national assembly, and so on. Personally,
I do not think these shallow objections deserve any
notice ; but whoever cares to know how little of
substance there is in them should read Dr.
Hancock's comments thereon. He shows them to
be evidence of either ignorance or want of due consideration. He might have added that they are, in
some instances, evidence of the old English animus
which would, if possible, deny the existence of the
Sechhus Mōr itself, and in fact does so by represent-

ing that Ireland was wholly without law until English law was introduced. Many generations of English children have been deliberately taught this falsehood at school, and when they have grown up the fact that a thing is respectable and Irish is quite sufficient proof for them that it does not exist at all. It is the very existence of the Senchus Mōr and of our beautiful illuminated manuscripts that confounds such people, and therefore irritates them. Knowing that themselves cannot err, they feel that the facts are perverse and have got wrong somehow. They would willingly lavish money digging for such things in the *débris* of Greece or in the sands of Egypt, but if told of its existence in Ireland they duly shrug their shoulders and proceed to doubt and criticise instead of taking the trouble to learn. A similar modification and codification of laws took place in Gaul about a quarter of a century earlier than in Ireland ; and we have already observed that more than a century and a half later Saint Augustine had the scraps of Saxon laws that existed in Kent collected, arranged, and modified.

I find it stated that after the laws had been collected and revised by the Committee of Nine, they did not *ipso facto* take effect in their altered state until sanctioned by the national assembly. No authority is given for this statement, nor have I met with any in the Senchus Mōr itself. But since without a positive national ratification and acceptance, although the changes effected were not such as could be called revolutionary, they might be disputed in some quarter. As nothing of this sort appears to have occurred, and as the universal acceptance and stability of the alterations were essential to the success of Saint Patrick's work, there is little doubt that he took the obvious precaution of having the alterations sanctioned in the most formal and effectual manner then known, namely, by a great assembly. Whether the second assembly was a special one of an unusual character like the first, or the ordinary Feis of Tara, there is no record to show.

CHAPTER IV.

LEGISLATIVE ASSEMBLIES.

SECTION I.

INTRODUCTORY.

OME historical writers go so far as to say that there was an entire absence of legislative power in ancient Ireland. This is quite too sweeping, and wholly inconsistent with the ascertained facts of the period in which we are mainly interested, the period, namely, of the compilation of the Brehon code. But, unfortunately, it is applicable to the nation, though not quite so to the clan, at a subsequent period when the national assembly had ceased to meet. Authors who appear to be better informed maintain that there were five different sorts of legislative assemblies in ancient Ireland, some of them

being for national, some for provincial, and some
for local or tribal purposes. No one has yet
sufficiently investigated the subject to be able to
set forth with precision what the constitutions,
duties and powers of those assemblies were.

The idea of *making* laws does not appear to be
natural to primitive man. This is proved by the
early history of many nations gleaned with the
greatest care; though a good deal that is theoretical
might be advanced to the contrary. The prevailing
sentiment of primitive races always has been, and
still is, that laws handed down from remote antiquity
should not be meddled with. The object of the long
and apologetic preambles of old English Acts of
Parliament was to soothe this sentiment and reconcile it to the changes about to be enacted. So long
as such a sentiment prevails, and to its extent, there
is a reluctance to tamper with laws. I cannot say
how far this sentiment prevailed in Ireland, but
it is certain to have existed to some extent; and
what is given as a Gaelic proverb would go to
support it—"The old rule transcends the new
knowledge." But quite apart from this sentiment,
the simple life of the people, the system of *clan* and
fine, with its network of rights conferred and duties
imposed, and the just character of the existing laws
must have reduced to a minimum the necessity for
direct law-making.

When nations which had not fallen under subjection to a despotism had arrived at the idea of making
and altering their laws, they at first met in public

assembly and did it by direct vote of the free and qualified citizens, those citizens being on such occasions, in some nations, armed and clashing their arms in token of final assent. Later on when some system of representation or delegation had been devised, the assemblies so formed were usually given power, not only to make and alter the laws, but to enforce them and also to apply them judicially, and to determine whether they had or had not been observed or violated. There being little direct *making* of new law, but chiefly a gradual adaptation and blending in the course of administration, there was no clearly marked distinction between legislative, executive, and judicial functions. All those functions were discharged, for instance, by the Saxon Witan; and it was from such a state of things, though in very different circumstances, that the English Star Chamber arose. The judicial powers of the House of Lords and of the Privy Council of the present day come, through various winding ways, from the same source. These observations apply so generally to other nations that one would expect to find traces of a similar evolution in Ireland; yet those who have read Irish manuscripts most extensively assure us that, so far as they have been able to discover, the Irish always had courts of justice quite distinct from their legislative assemblies. Irish courts of justice appear to have attained a far more advanced stage of development than Irish legislative assemblies. The converse of this would be true of ancient Rome, for instance. But some of the Irish assemblies, perhaps all, were still much more than legislative; or rather the work of legislation does not appear to have been the sole, or even the principal, duty of any of them. In pagan times, at all events, their primary and principal duties were of a semi-religious character, with legislative, executive, administrative, and social duties superadded as occasion arose. And possibly the introduction of Christianity effected no greater change in the assemblies than the elimination of the old religious observances. Some of the assemblies were constituted mainly of the Flaiths, or nobles, with a small number of other distinguished men, and in this respect may be said to have resembled the present House of Peers. A national assembly of this character met at Tara, and there was in each provincial kingdom an assembly constituted on the same exclusive model. Some of the assemblies, especially those that were local, were probably constituted of as many heads of families of the Céile, or freehold class, as chose to attend them, the clan system conferring the qualification, and there being no other form of election.

The wilful disturbance of any lawfully constituted public assembly, national or local, was one of the few things for which a fine was not considered adequate punishment; the penalty was death.

SECTION II.

THE FEIS OF TARA.

HE most important of all the ancient assemblies was the Feis of Tara. It is said by some to have been founded, in the year of the world 3884, by King Ollamh Fodhla, whose name means Sage of Ireland, and whose reign was so propitious that "it was difficult for the stalk to bear its corn in his reign." Others say the Feis originated in funeral games. The truth probably is, that it originated in funeral games, and was turned to the other purposes by Ollamh Fodhla. At all events, a national assembly was held at Tara from a very early period down to A.D. 560, when the last was held there under King Dermot, son of Fergus.

The Feis of Tara was an assembly of the leading

men of the whole island—kings, tanists, flaiths,
warriors, brehons, chief poets, &c.—not a meeting
of all classes of society. It was not ambulatory,
like the English national assembly of later times,
held now in one place, now in another, wherever
the king happened to be ; nor was it haphazard like
that by which Magna Carta was adopted. Its
constitution and its place of meeting were fixed,
and its times of meeting fairly regular. It met at
Tara every third year, three days before the 1st of
November, and it continued in session three days
after the 1st of November. Thus its ordinary
session lasted for seven days. For some time before
it ceased, however, it had been summoned less
frequently.

There was an important pagan festival observed
all over the country on the feast of Belltainé, which
was the 1st of May; and at Tara it was the
occasion of an assembly lasting for some days.
But those assembled on this occasion seem to
have been brought together mainly by religious and
social motives and the attractions of the royal
court.

Dr. Joyce is of opinion that some of the ancient
Irish national assemblies did directly enact laws,
but that the Feis of Tara was not one of these ; and
he doubts that the Feis was convened to enact laws,
and says there is no ancient authority for holding
that it was. Other authorities do not agree with
Dr. Joyce in this latter view, and I find himself
speaking in another place of the summoning of the

Feis on "some urgent occasion." An assembly
which was summoned on an urgent occasion, when
there were serious matters to be considered and
dealt with, was certainly summoned for some
practical purpose, and must have been in some
sense the Great Council of the Nation; and if it
did not enact laws, it must have deliberated on
national affairs with effect, which is a near approach
to law-making. In a poem, written in the tenth
century, the Feis is spoken of as having been convened "to preserve laws and rules." Edward
O'Reilly, the Gaelic scholar, calls the Feis "a
parliament." It may be that neither the Feis of
Tara nor the other assemblies were convened for
the express purpose of *making* new laws, or ever
professed *to make* new laws, but only to promulgate,
reaffirm, retrench, modify or otherwise affect laws
long known but for some temporary or partial or
local reason suspended, or to extend to the whole
kingdom some advantageous local custom, or to
correct or abrogate some vicious custom, or to
enforce uniformity among the brehons in case of
conflicting judicial interpretation, or to restrain on
the ground of some local or temporary hardship the
strict enforcement of a law otherwise just. There are
countless things like these which a national assembly
could do well, and in doing which it would be
modifying the law; and although it never called
itself a legislative assembly, and never claimed *to
make* laws, we are still quite justified in calling its
acts legislative. While many eminent authorities

hold that the Feis of Tara did these things, Dr. Joyce's view cannot be accepted as final.

Among the other duties performed at the Feis was one of some importance even now, but of infinitely more then, because on it the title to rank, property, and privileges largely depended. This was the comparing and checking of the local pedigrees with each other, and with the Monarch's Book, or Register, kept at Tara. Analogous duties are now divided between the offices of the Herald and the Registrar-General.

King Dermot died in A.D. 563 (or 565), and after his death no Ard-Rīg resided at Tara. No separate Ard-Rīg was any more appointed with the kingdom of Meath for his mensal. One of the provincial kings usually assumed the office, or at least the title, retaining and residing in his own province. Tara was deserted, and no place for holding a national assembly was ever substituted. To the time from this date onward, the saying applies that there was no central legislative authority acting for the whole island. Once after the reign of Dermot a national assembly, or convention, was held at Tara, but although legislative it can hardly be called the Feis. It was held in the reign of the monarch Loingseach about A.D. 697; and at the instance of Saint Adamnan a law was adopted which, among other things, freed women from liability to military service, and prohibited their presence in battle.

After the abandonment of Tara as a royal residence, and the consequent discontinuance of a

national assembly, it can hardly be said that one
concrete state, broad and national in basis and con-
centrated in executive power, existed in Ireland. As
though Tara had been the vivifying sun of true
national life, a summons or word of command from
any other source never could be and never was
frankly recognised as the voice of the Ard-Rīg,
never could and never did inspire the old generous
patriotism, but often inspired bitter jealousy of
(as was deemed) a local usurper in the person of the
nominal Ard-Rīg, a desire to dispute his title if
possible, and to set up a rival. Many holders of
the office after Dermot's time are marked kings
" with opposition " ; and though this opposition was
not successful, its existence had a disintegrating
effect among the people, and in law actually reduced
the king's status and rights in certain cases. True
national unity, and with it true national security,
was at an end. The nation was divided into a large
number of small isolated communities called *Tuaths*,
the territorial extent of which is in many cases
represented by the modern baronies. These communities had some of the characteristics of states,
and fancied themselves such, but were in reality
fragments of a nation falling asunder, and were
doomed to become political ruins if not re-united.
Small nationalities are dear to the Spirit of Freedom,
but she loves not the aimless subdivision of a nation
that is really one in race and interest. There always
had been much independence of action in the several
tuaths ; and this was well so long as it originated

in worthy aims, or in wholesome and honest rivalry,
and could be subordinated at once to the interests
of the tuath, and of the nation by the controlling
and assimilating influence of a supreme central
authority. But once that authority ceased to exist
at Tara it *de facto* ceased to have any existence; the
several tuaths pursued what they deemed their
several interests, keen in the assertion of a puny
autonomy but blind and indifferent to the common
national interest; and the country sank into the
condition of England under what is called the
Heptarchy, when the petty Saxon kingdoms were
so independent that they were almost constantly at
war with each other.

It is thought that one of the events which had
most influence in bringing about the consolidation
of England was the reduction of the Church there
to a single national Church by Theodore of Tarsus,
when Archbishop of Canterbury, in the latter part of
seventh century. Before his time, the territorial
limits of ecclesiastical jurisdiction had varied and
shifted with the varying fortunes of the little
kingdoms. He fixed permanently the limits of
spiritual jurisdiction, and subjected the Church
throughout England to one central authority. Some
such service would then have been a boon of in-
estimable value to Ireland, even if it had come from
foreign lands; for while over-centralisation is undoubtedly a great evil, so much of it as is necessary
to inspire a common patriotism and prevent the
degradation of local rivalry to sordid jealousy is as

undoubtedly a great good. It happened that the Church in Ireland exerted no such influence and afforded no such example, for it had from the beginning accommodated itself to the genius of the people to the extent of assuming somewhat of a clannish complexion without the national organism and outward visible bond with which we are now familiar. Each clan aimed at being self-provided, self-contained, and self-existing in every respect, spiritual and temporal. It built small churches, monasteries, and schools; endowed them with lands, stock, and all necessaries, in the same generous manner in which, in previous generations, it had provided for the Druids and other learned men; it dedicated, as a rule, every first-born son to the Church; and it retained to itself the right of succession to all posts, clerical and lay, so long as it possessed qualified persons. Indeed, the requirement of qualification can hardly have been always very rigorously insisted upon, inasmuch as positions of great importance were in many instances filled for successive generations by members of the same family, as though in a sense hereditary. This latter feature, however, was due to a certain general tendency, which we shall have a more suitable occasion to notice.

The clan had its bishop too, or an abbot having episcopal faculties; and so far as territorial jurisdiction was known at all his was coterminus with that of the clan. The bond between those pastors seems to have been of a very vague character, the chief

5 .

connecting link apparently being the purely spiritual one of a common faith. The successor of Saint Patrick was always Primate, and always held in special reverence over the whole country. The occupant of that position could have done for Ireland what Theodore did for England ; but being usually a man of Irish training, and seeing things as he had been accustomed to see them and with Irish eyes, the necessity for organising the Church on the modern principle does not appear to have occurred to him with sufficient force to call forth effective action in its attainment until a later time, just when the nation had become incapable of profiting by the example.

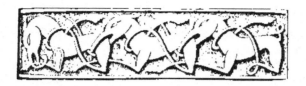

SECTION III.

TAILLTENN AND UISNEACH.

NOTHER very celebrated national assembly was that held for many centuries at Tailltenn on the Blackwater in Meath. It was a general assembly of the people— that is to say, not restricted to men of rank and distinction like that at Tara. It was held annually about the beginning of August. It also originated in funeral games, or rites; but its subsequent purposes were even more manifold than those of the assembly at Tara, and they varied from time to time. They always included the social and political; and, as at all the great assemblies, the laws were always proclaimed anew—that is, read aloud in public that they might not be forgotten, and any changes in them carefully explained to those present. The last of the regular assemblies at

Tailltenn was held under King Roderick O'Connor in A.D. 1168.

The Hill of Uisneach, in Westmeath, was, in pagan times, the site of a national assembly distinctly legislative in character. It was at one such assembly, held there about one hundred years before the birth of Christ, that a uniform law of distress for the whole country was adopted. Uisneach has been the site of many political conferences since then, but I have met with no account of an assembly there, purely legislative, since the nation became Christian.

SECTION IV.

F local assemblies, the Aenach appears to have been the most generally important. *Aenach* is the word now translated *fair*, and is, in fact, the present Irish term for a cattle - fair. But though some such fairs originated in aenachs, they bear very little resemblance to the original. Fair is no translation of the word, but is one of those things which one would rather have expressed differently. Aenach means, first, an assembly; second, a hill, from assemblies meeting on hills; third, a cattle-fair, from such fairs springing up where aenachs once were held. Wherever an aenach was held a fair sprang up, but the latter was purely a consequential and collateral adjunct to the former. The aenach proper was an assembly of all the people of a

district, without distinction of rank, and apparently
without distinction of clan. Some were held an-
nually, others triennially. Originating, like all
the other Irish assemblies, in pagan funeral or
commemorative rites, the aenach continued even
in Christian times to meet in a cemetery. There
is no definite statement that the aenach enacted
laws ; but one of the many objects of the
assembly was that the laws might be published,
and where this was done the effect of the laws
may have been in some way modified. The
aenach was also taken advantage of for holding a
high court of justice for the trial of appeals and
cases of special difficulty, a Church synod in
Christian times, a place for musical and bardic
contests, for the recitation of martial and other
poetry and family pedigrees, a weapon-show or
sort of military review, feats of arms, horse-racing,
athletic sports, and all the games of the time, and,
of course, for the distribution of honours and prizes
amongst the successful competitors. So far the
assembly might be considered the aenach proper.
But all these proceedings, and the multitude of
people they brought together and detained in one
place for a couple of days, rendered a market for
refreshments necessary ; and this developed into
a market for all kinds of wares and produce and
for cattle. Owing to the scarcity of towns and
shops in those days, this incidental feature of the
aenach was found very convenient ; and it grew to
such an extent that it ultimately overshadowed the

primary purposes of the aenach, and furnished a
practical if not an etymological reason for translating the word into *fair*.   For the commercial
purposes of the fair those meetings were frequented
by merchants, Irish and foreign, and a brief but
vigorous trade was carried on.

Aenachs were held in many places throughout the
country, and the word still forms part of the names
of a number of places, the best known in this respect
being Nenagh.   But the accident of retaining the
name is no indication of the relative importance of
the different aenachs held in those places.   For they
did differ greatly in importance.   The aenach of
Carman was for a long time one of the most celebrated in the South of Ireland.   Carman was a place
near the site of the present town of Wexford, and,
I believe, is the Irish name of that town.   The last
aenach was held there in A.D. 1033, under Donnchadh
MacGillaphadraig, Chief of Ossory, who was King
of Leinster then.   Greek merchants are spoken of
as having attended the aenach of Carman for commercial purposes.

SECTION V.

THE TRIBAL ASSEMBLIES.

ACH clan had two local assemblies of its own for the transaction of its ordinary business, legislative and administrative. These were the authoritative fountains of urradhus law. One was called the *Cuirmtig* (pronounced *Coorthy*), and was probably open to all clansmen who paid tribute. In it, for the most part, new proposals originated. The other was called the *Dal*, and appears to have been open only to heads of septs; possibly to heads of *fines* also. *Dal* means a tribe or division of a race, but it had also the special meaning of an assembly representing and acting for the tribe. It was a sort of local second chamber, in which bills passed in the first had to be ratified before they became legally binding. Each clan had also a further assembly

56

called a Tocomra. This was the assembly in which
the king or chief or tanist was elected. So far as
I can discover it consisted of the same persons as
the *Dal*; but it was summoned by the *Bruigh-fer*,
or *Biadhtach* (pronounced *Beetagh*), and met in his
house. This house was not the private property of
this officer, but was considered somewhat as a public
hall belonging to the clan, and used as occasion
required for clan purposes. The Bruigh-fer, or
Biadhtach, was its occupant and keeper and a clan
official appointed and empowered to discharge
various duties of high importance. Besides summoning the assembly just mentioned, he was bound
to entertain the king, bishop, bard, judge, and some
other public functionaries of the clan who were
privileged to claim entertainment for themselves
and a number of attendants fixed in each case by
the law. He was also bound to entertain when
required, on behalf of the clan, friendly visitors, if for
any reason the king or chief could not conveniently
do so ; and he was under certain legal obligations to
all belated travellers who passed by the way. In
fact he may be called a public hospitaler, and this
is almost the literal signification of the word
Biadhtach. To enable him to comply with these
extensive requirements, he was allowed about five
hundred acres of free land, besides various personal
privileges ; and he was, by virtue of his office,
a magistrate empowered to administer justice in
certain cases. There were many special provisions
in the law for the protection of himself and his

official property, for he and his house were rightly regarded as an important public institution. He was fancifully supposed to have five doors to his house, facing in different directions, always a pot of meat boiling, and cattle and pigs on the premises fat enough for killing.

In later centuries ballybetagh, so named from this officer, came to mean among the English in Ireland a sort of rough measure of land equal to about five hundred acres.

CHAPTER V.

CLASSIFICATION OF SOCIETY.

SECTION I.

INTRODUCTORY.

ERSONAL rights of the political and social order were in ancient Ireland arranged upon a graduated scale of status, and society was divided into a great number of classes, or grades, quite distinct in many respects according to the position they occupied on this scale. One of the Gaelic commentators of the Middle Ages says, among other things, " The world was at an equality until the Senchus Mōr was written." That part of his statement may be disregarded.

At all events, I go on the assumption that it is incorrect; nor do I deem it necessary to state my reasons. For our present purpose, however, ancient Irish society may conveniently be divided into six general classes—(1) the kings of various grades; (2) the professional classes; (3) the flaiths, who constituted a sort of official nobility; (4) freemen possessing property; (5) freemen possessing none (or very little); and (6) the non-free classes. But although quite distinct, these classes were not utterly exclusive *castes* such as we read of in Eastern countries. It was possible for persons to rise (or sink, as the case might be) from one class to another. Rank and office meant nearly the same thing; or perhaps it would be more correct to say that wealth, rank, office, power and responsibility were considered as co-ordinate ingredients of status, and therefore always vested in the same persons proportionately according to their respective positions from the king downwards. Progress from one rank to another was no doubt effected in a variety of ways, as by duly qualifying for a learned profession, by displaying conspicuous valour, conspicuous skill in some department, the performance of some signal service to the community, and *the possession of wealth.* The first mentioned qualifications were personal and of immediate effect; this latter one was proprietorial and not always immediate. Its frank recognition shows that our ancestors were of a far more practical turn of mind than they now generally get credit for.

Their complex political, social, and military system
was avowedly based on the possession of wealth to
even a greater extent than the system founded at
Rome by Servius Tullius. The effect of wealth in
this respect was arranged and calculated frankly
upon fixed rules, and not left uncertain and indefinite as is now generally the case. Such a system
at least furnished an incentive to thrift and industry.
Every clansman was eligible, provided he possessed
sufficient property, and had not forfeited his right by
crime, to become an Aire (pronounced *Arra*); if he
owned the qualifying property of a Flaith, and his
family had owned that property for three generations,
he might become a Flaith ; and a Flaith was always
eligible for the highest office in the state. On the
other hand, loss of wealth below a given amount involved loss of the status to which that amount corresponded. The Irish system had this advantage over
the Roman system, that when persons of an inferior
grade had not sufficient property individually to
qualify for the full rights of citizenship, as the rights
of suing, of being jurors, witnesses, sureties, &c., a
number of them might combine, form a guild or
partnership, take a piece of land (presumably waste
land), and this joint property, after they had cultivated it for ten years and fenced it off, would give a
qualification for one of them to become an Aire, with
all rights of citizenship and power to act for the
partnership without external assistance. A similar
right of forming partnerships was given to artisans
and others who lived by handicrafts and such forms

of industry; and having combined, they could choose
from among themselves a person to become an aire,
act for them, and enjoy full rights of citizenship on
their behalf.   These partnerships, or guilds, were a
very important economic feature in ancient Ireland.
Each rank in the ascending scale brought to the man
who had reached it an expansion of liberty, an
accession of rights and privileges, and a corresponding increase of liabilities.   Also the fines
recoverable in case of injury depended upon rank;
and rank depended largely upon wealth.

There are indications that the different classes
were distinguished by the colours of their dress; but
there is no trace of any one having been punished for
having violated this rule, and I think we shall not
be far wrong in concluding that the rule strictly
applied only to public occasions, that it was enforced
rather by pride than by enactment, and that its
extension to private life was due not so much to
either of these causes as to convenience.

Let us now consider the various classes in the
order named.

SECTION II.

THE KINGS.

ÆSAR says that in Gaul some of the states were ruled by senates, with no individual holding the office of head of the state. But in nearly every case he appears to have found aspirants to that position, the sons or descendants of deposed kings; and if in any case he found neither a king nor an aspirant, the fact may have been due to some accidental cause, and without inquiring sufficiently he may have assumed what he as a Roman would expect. At all events, such a state of things does not appear to have at any time existed in Ireland or in any part of it. The Irish always had a man, not an assembly, at the head of the state, and the system

of electing a Tanist while the holder of the office
was living, in addition to its making for peace on the
demise of the crown, made an interregnum of more
rare occurrence than in countries which had not
provided a Tanist in advance. Ireland has on a few
occasions been ruled by two monarchs jointly; and
for a few years after the death of Malachy the
Second, in the eleventh century, it was ruled by two
judges who were not kings. But these were exceptional occurrences, and beyond them kingly rule was
quite uniform.

The word *Cing* occurs in the Gaelic manuscripts
as the equivalent of *Rīg;* but *Rīg* (pronounced *Reeh*)
is the term generally employed. It is cognate with
the Latin *Reg-s* = *Rex.* It did not designate precisely the same class of official as the word *king* now
does. Primarily, and above all things, the rīg was
the head and representative of his race and clan, the
members of which were rather his kindred whose
interests it was his duty to serve than subjects to be
ruled ; and the word *rīg* being considered as a generic
term, there was no inconsistency in several ranks
or classes of rīgs flourishing at the same time and
forming a sort of hierarchy, the members of which
were mutually dependent on each other. Our
ancestors aimed, in theory at least, at interde-
pendence in all departments.

The lowest *oirrīg, regulus,* or sub-king was the
Rīg-Tuatha, a king of one tuath, or district, the
people of which formed one organic state. As
already observed, these tuaths were very numerous,

but sometimes two or three of them that were nearly related had but one king. And where there were separate rulers, the term *rīg* was by no means rigorously adhered to. Various other descriptive terms were employed; but the word *rīg* is simple and convenient for our purpose.

The next in rank was the Rīg-Mōr-Tuatha. He was a ruler of a number of united tuaths, each of which might have a rīg-tuatha of its own, subject in some respects to the Rīg-Mōr-Tuatha.

The next class of king was called the Rīg-Cuicidh, a word implying that he had five rīg-mōr-tuathas under him, each of whom in turn might have three, four, or more rīg-tuaths under him. This was the rank of the provincial king.

So long as the Ard-Rīg resided at Tara he may be considered, by reason of his exceptional privileges, to have formed a separate rank of royalty, or rather its head; but after the abandonment of Tara, since the Ard-Rīg was rarely able to enforce his rights, he may be considered as belonging to the class of the provincial kings.

The king of each tuath owed allegiance and tribute to the Rīg-Mōr-Tuatha; the latter owed allegiance and tribute to the Rīg-Cuicidh; and the Rīg-Cuicidh owed allegiance and tribute to the Ard-Rīg. The special branch of law affecting the allegiance in each case, the amount of the tribute, the amount to be returned by the recipient of the tribute, and other constitutional matters, was contained in the *Psalter of Tara* as drawn up under the direction of King

6

Cormac, and also in the ancient *Book of Rights* (if this be a different work); and much on the same subjects will be found in a later *Book of Rights* which still exists and has been translated by O'Donovan. The prerogatives, privileges, duties, and liabilities of the various kings within their own territories are fully laid down in the course of the general law; and when the clan system was in an efficient condition, so many forces acted in aid of the law, and a neglect of official duty affected so many persons that, in ordinary times of peace, such neglect must have been rare. The king was not in any sense the maker of the law, but its officer, and so limited and hemmed round in his office, and so dependent on his clan, that it was easier and safer for him to conform to the intention of the law and promote the welfare of his people than to become either negligent or despotic.

The office of Rīg, of whatever rank, was always elective, as was the office of king anciently among the Saxons. But the choice was restricted by custom in the case of the Ard-Rīg and provincial kings to a narrow circle of the flaith class called the *Riogh-dhamhna* or *Damna Rīg* (=*Materia Principum*), the members of which were required to undergo a very careful training, mental and physical. It was therefore as a rule confined to the family in possession. So long as there was an eligible member of that family, the kingship may be said to have been practically hereditary in that family, but not in any particular member of it. An eldest son did not succeed merely because his father had been king, if there was an uncle, nephew, brother, cousin, or other member of the Damna Rīg better fit for the position ; and the Tanist was usually such a relative, and not a son. The same rules applied to the election of sub-kings, but being in rank not so far removed from the flaiths the distinctions were not so marked, and if the family in possession failed, the flaith best qualified was eligible. The law on the subject is expressed in the following words : " Every head defends its members if it be a goodly head, of good deeds, of good morals, exempt, affluent, and capable. The body of every head is his tribe, for there is no body without a head. The head of every tribe, according to the people, should be the man of the tribe who is most experienced, the most noble, the most wealthy, the most wise, the most learned, the most truly popular, the most powerful to oppose, the most steadfast to sue for profits and to be sued for losses." No person not of age, stupid, blind, deaf, deformed, or otherwise defective in mind or body, or for any reason whatsoever unfit to discharge the duties of the public position, or unfit worthily to represent the manhood of the community, could be chosen for king or could hold the kingship ; even a blemish on the face was a disqualification. Here were requirements enough, positive and negative, which not every man could satisfy. The method of choosing the king was not fully one of merit, nor fully elective, nor fully heredi-tary, but a combination of all three : and on the

whole the office resembled as much that of president
of a republic as it did that of a modern king.

The Ard-Rīg was not elected by the people at
large, but by the sub-kings and flaiths of all Ireland,
the same men who constituted the Feis of Tara.
The provincial kings were elected by the flaiths and
aires of their respective provinces. The king of a
tuath was elected by the flaiths, aires, and probably
all heads of families in the tuath. The immediate
position to which the person was elected in each case
was usually that of Tanaiste or Tanist (=Second),
the king being living. The Tanist was a successor
or heir-presumptive elected before his time. He
sometimes acted as a sort of vice-president while the
king lived. As soon as he in his turn became king,
a new tanist was elected, so that there was rarely a
direct election to the office of king.

The king was, of course, by virtue of his office,
head of the State in general, whether in arms or in
peace. He was the fountain of honour and of
justice, and one of his duties was to appoint a brehon
to administer law in his district. He had himself,
in ordinary times, some magisterial jurisdiction.
King Cormac, for example, is spoken of as a
"righteous judge," and all kings are spoken of as
hearing cases and pronouncing judgments. The
nature or extent of this jurisdiction is not clearly
stated, but I think it had to do mainly with criminal
law, especially treason and the kindred crimes. If
from any cause there was in his district no brehon,
or the brehon was incapacitated, the king himself

was bound to act as judge in cases calling for immediate settlement,

Wealth is mentioned among the qualifications for
the kingly office, but in addition to his private wealth
a considerable amount of land was set apart for the
use of every holder of the office, what was deemed
sufficient to support the dignity and bear the expenses connected with it.   On this land there was
always a *dun.*   A provincial king usually had several
mensals of this nature with a dun on each.   " The
residence of a king is always a dun, and there is no
dun without a king."

SECTION III.

PROFESSIONAL MEN.

Sub-Section 1.—Preliminary.

ROFESSIONAL men next demand our attention, and of these especially the Brehons. The laws were administered in Ireland by brehons, so called while so engaged. It is not clear that there was in early times, as there was in later, a distinct order of men so engaged and not otherwise—judges and nothing else, and there is some reason for thinking that this was an after-growth. In the older manuscripts the words *druid*, *bard*, and *brehon* appear to be applied to the same persons interchangeably and as if synonymous.

The terms are, however, not synonymous, and never were, even when applied to the same person. One person being a very learned man might be all three; and probably this was so sometimes, and was always looked for in pre-Christian times. But, of course, its continuance was neither necessary nor possible. In some of the manuscripts it is said that legal jurisdiction was vested in the bards, the "just bards" are spoken of as custodians of the law, and the old law itself is called by a name which may be translated "Bardic Law." Further, a man who administered the law judicially, whether bard or druid or neither, is called a *Breitheam* or judge; genitive *Breitheamhuin*, pronounced *Brehon* (another instance of the adaptation to English of the genitive of a Gaelic word). Here we have three apparently different classes of men connected with the law in some way; but in what that connection consisted, and what were their mutual relations, or rather their actual distinctions, is not clearly stated.

Sub-Section 2.—*The Druids.*

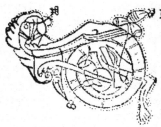RUIDS next claim consideration. One modern writer tells us that the Druids were "magicians and nothing more." Magicians, yes; "and nothing more" must be rejected. The popular view of what they were is more nearly accurate than this. The druids were much more. They were above all things the priests of such religion as existed; and in that character were quite as highly venerated and as influential in Ireland as Cæsar found them in Gaul. Their religion, if their many strange and conflicting views and practices may be considered as one system and called a religion, was, to our minds, degraded and degrading, and their ceremonies may appear to us silly or worse; we may think Crom Cruach very unworthy of worship;

but what does all this matter if that religion
was dear to the people as the essence of a spiritual
life and the prime requisite for attaining eternal
happiness and glory, and if it yielded to its
adherents any of the consolations which religion
affords and for which the human heart yearns? It
cannot be doubted that in Ireland, as in Gaul, the
most learned, the most sage, and the most virtuous
men of the nation were druids or priests of that
religion. Their superior learning enabled them to
become more than priests; magicians if you will,
but certainly philosophers, astronomers, judges,
bards, literary men, musicians, physicians, seers or
diviners of future events, and many other things,
and may have given them a choice, almost a
monopoly, of all the offices which required learning.
Their magic consisted mainly in their superior knowledge in times of general simplicity; and I think
they deserve to be called a learned priesthood. In
those circumstances most of the brehons, perhaps
nearly all, were druids; but all druids were not
brehons, for the office of brehon was but one of a
choice of accessory offices which their learning
opened to the druids. This seems to account
sufficiently for the connection of the druids with
the law, and for the apparent opinion of the writers
of old that the terms druid and brehon might be
used interchangeably.

It is impossible now to determine whether at
any time the office of brehon was restricted to the
druids as an exclusive legal priesthood. Probably

there never was a positive restriction, but only the
practical one involved in the requirement of learning, which few laymen could then satisfy. But
the administration of the law not being the special
function of the druids as such, but only a sort of
secondary string to their bow, they may be supposed
to have bestowed more attention upon whatever
their special function was than upon law. The
law remained in the Bearla Feini, the old classical
Gaelic in which it had been originally composed,
and constituted a large and important part of the
Filidecht or higher academic course through which
both druids and bards should pass, and in which
they should attain a certain standard of proficiency
before being admitted to their respective professions.
As that old language gradually became antiquated
the laws became less accessible and less intelligible
to others than those learned men; and yet the
school knowledge of it, which had sufficed for them
and was little more than an accomplishment, did not
always enable them to deal satisfactorily with the
legal difficulties of everyday life. It is easy to conceive
that in such circumstances the law may sometimes
have failed in its primary object of bringing justice
home to the people. An evident want arose. The
combined effect of the negligence of those two classes
of men and the growing importance of law must
have made it clear that the administration of justice
ought not to be secondary to anything, but deserved
the special and exclusive study of a distinct profession. To this profession laymen applied themselves

in increasing numbers as the druids withdrew, until the administration of the law had got almost wholly into non-sacerdotal hands. Not being occupied with religion or with any other profession, nor hampered with the trivial formalities which the sacerdotal mind has always been so prone to create and magnify, these men could breathe a freer air, enter more sympathetically into the views and feelings of both parties to a suit, and arrive at a decision more satisfactory to both, than is as a rule possible to men who, though in the world, are best when they are not of it.

In Rome also the pagan priests were the earliest judges and custodians of the law. They greatly hampered its justice and its efficiency by the invention of useless technicalities, until at length, in 451 B.C., the Romans resolved to reduce their laws into a written and fixed form, and called upon the priests to produce the laws for that purpose; when, lo, it was found that the priests, after all, really had no substantive laws to produce, that they had completely lost what it had been their business and their pretence to guard, and had guarded nothing but their own technical inventions, mainly concerned with mere procedure (or its prevention), and mainly detrimental to the free flow of justice. Hence the Romans in drawing up their Twelve Tables were obliged to resort to laymen of common-sense, and even to consult neighbouring nations as to the very rudiments of law.

Sub-Section 3.—*The Bards.*

N OW with regard to the *Files* or Bards. They did not, like the druids, become extinct on the extirpation of paganism, but continued to flourish and to form an important class down to modern times. They were anciently much more than the present popular conception of them implies, for they were the historians, genealogists, teachers, and literary men of the nation, some of them also being druids and some judges; but as regards the bards of Christian times, after the monks had taken learning and teaching under their special care, the present conception of the bards is fairly accurate, and therefore their connection with law is not at first sight obvious. Little or no such connection continued to exist, and the presence of the bards in battle and their thrilling

writings relative thereto remind one more of the
war correspondents of our own time than of
lawyers. Anciently some of them were judges
in addition to being bards, as we have seen in
the case of Dubhthach; but these instances were
few even then, and not at all sufficient to explain
the intimate connection between the bards and the
older law. The secret of that connection lies elsewhere. Their chief connection with law was not
in the character of judges, but in their proper
character of bards. In this their true character
there was then a use for them amounting almost
to necessity. Accustomed as we are to writing,
printing, and other modes of preserving expressions
of thought, we are liable to forget that the laws we
are considering originated when those arts were
unknown, when in northern climates men preserved
their learning in their heads instead of on their
shelves, and communicated it by their tongues
instead of by ink and paper. Verse always has
been, and still is, easily committed to memory and
retained there; and the more harmonious it is, the
more effective and reliable for this purpose. To
give this quality to things of value, as law, history,
and genealogy, not to speak of pure literature, to
which this quality was then natural, was in such a
time as important a service as a bard could render
to his nation. It imprinted those things, not on
paper, but on brains; fixed them in heads where
otherwise they would not abide, and rendered them
capable of being transmitted from person to person,

from clan to clan, from generation to generation,
from times far beyond the reach of history until
well into historic times. This use of poetry was
clearly very important, and hence the originals of
almost all our very early manuscripts, on law as
well as on other subjects, were in verse. It was
the duty of the bards to reduce the laws into
rhythmical form, and they retained that function
in their hands for some time after the actual necessity for it had ceased to exist. Nothing but a sense
of duty could induce a body of learned men to take
such wonderful trouble with a subject so unattrac-
tive and unpromising. This fully accounts for the
connection of the bards with our ancient law and
explains the sense in which they were its custodians;
and it also accounts for the abnormal development
of the bardic profession in Ireland, and for the extraordinary amount of archaic Gaelic literature preserved.
The combined effect of metre and rhyme was to
render tradition at once easy and reliable. To take
the Senchus Mōr for example, though now arranged
prose-like on the paper, portions of the text are in
regular verse ; not merely in metre like blank verse,
but in rhyme. The editors say that whether this is
due to the fact that two of the compilers of the
Senchus Mōr were poets, or to the fact that the
pre-existing laws of Ireland were mostly in rhyme,
or partly to both these causes, is an open question.
Perhaps so. I think most students of the subject
will for themselves consider the question as closed,
and feel quite satisfied that the ancient laws of

Ireland were mostly in rhyme, or in an alliterative assonance having all the properties of rhyme for ar˙ and memory, from necessity before the art of writing was known, and from the unexhausted force of a long-established usage after that art had become known. The art of writing became known to some extent in Ireland about the first Christian century, or perhaps a little earlier; its practice was encouraged and extended under King Cormac, in the third century, and from his time downwards; but it was not until the introduction of Christianity in the fifth century that writing became general. During this period, at all events, the time-honoured custom of making and retaining the laws in rhyme undoubtedly held its ground; so that not alone did the compilers of the Senchus Mōr find the laws in rhyme, but they found the old usage still of quite sufficient force to require from themselves a semblance of reducing into rhyme any new laws then made, or modifications of the old. Rhymed laws were still the ideal aimed at. Accordingly there is reason to believe that the whole text of the Senchus Mōr, written in the fifth century, was in rhyme, and in the introduction, written at a later date, is included Dubhthach's fine poem as the most suitable introduction. This was probably the only introduction in the first instance, the work being then metrical and rhymed throughout. Wherever in the text the rhyme is now absent or broken the reader may conclude that there the various transcribers have been carrying on the operations I have endeavoured to explain. Finding it necessary to substitute new for obsolete words, and to translate some passages, and no longer a practical reason for reducing these emendations into rhyme, that ceremony was omitted, and thus while the law was simplified the verse was spoiled. The commentaries were not composed by bards at all, and so far as they are original they are not rhymed; but in them are frequently quoted fragments of traditional law for the purpose of driving home their conclusions, and such fragments are nearly all in rhymed metre.

The ancient cultivation of memory is one of the arts that have fallen into disrepute. It was carried, in other countries as well as in Ireland, to a degree of perfection now hardly credible. Nor were metre and alliteration, as subsidiary to it, peculiar to Ireland or to the Irish laws. The perfection attained in these was peculiar, and rhyme was peculiar. To the absence of this bardic perfection the poverty of other nations in archaic literature is due: to its presence our wealth in that respect is due. For other nations the remote past is a blank: for us it lives, mainly through the skill of the bards. The bards were liberally provided for by their contemporaries: we may enjoy their labour without having to pay for it.

Sub-Section 4.—*The Brehons.*

BEGINNING at the point where all three qualities were possessed and all three functions discharged by one man, the functions had expanded and become differentiated until they formed three separate professions, followed by three distinct classes of men—Druids, Bards, and Brehons—this last being the newest class in the order of development. So long as this development proceeded, the legal profession was perfectly open to every one who chose to study the law. A druid, or a bard, or a man who was neither, was perfectly free on qualifying himself to become a brehon. It is now impossible to fix the date at which this development was complete, and the brehons stood recognised as a professional class apart from druids and bards. It was probably complete in the first century of the Christian era,

7

certainly while Ireland was still wholly pagan ; and
there can be no doubt that it was a distinct advantage to the people and to the nation.

Later on a further change occurred (for it can
hardly be called a development), namely, the legal
profession, in common with most professions, arts
and callings, became to a large extent hereditary,
not by force of law, but by force of custom, and in
obedience to a general tendency of the times. There
never was a law in Ireland actually making any
profession or calling hereditary, or imposing any
restriction whatever on the natural right to learn
and practise what one pleased. The tendency was
spontaneous, or due to some general cause. In our
view it was a backward tendency. But that proves
nothing. The same may be said of many move-
ments far more modern. Our desire is to see, so
far as we can, our ancestors as they really were,
not to make them fit into theories of what they
should have been.

Whatever may have been the prevailing force in
making callings become hereditary, no doubt it was
materially assisted by the custom of rewarding
distinguished merit, and the performance of public
duties, with gifts of free land. This is a species of
reward not unknown in modern times ; but it was
obviously more convenient in ancient times when
there was little or no money with which to reward
men. Men occupying official positions, from the
king downwards, were provided with free lands.
Many of those positions were attainable only by

careful training and marked ability of the kind required. Bards, brehons, and other public officers, men distinguished in the healing and other arts, and in the handicrafts most important for the well-being and security of the community, were similarly provided for. A man having once acquired land in this way would have a strong motive for transmitting his profession to his children, since it was only by doing so he could transmit the land to them ; in addition to which, his own was the particular branch of knowledge which he could transmit, and they learn with least trouble and least expense. Here was a two-fold motive for making both the profession and the land attached to it hereditary.

In the case of the brehon's office this powerful cause did not operate alone. There were attached to the office manuscripts, in those early times of great value as legal documents, and perhaps still more precious privately as family heirlooms, the preservation of which, after his death, was an object of the most intense solicitude to every brehon worthy of the name. It was but human that a brehon should desire to entrust to his own offspring a charge so sacred, and but human that they, for his sake and for its own intrinsic value, should bestow more care upon such a trust than could be expected from strangers. In respect of the preservation of documents, and perhaps in other respects also, we of later times are much indebted to the hereditary custom, however that custom may in practice have militated against efficiency.

Still, although these causes must have acted powerfully, the office of brehon may, in obedience to the general tendency of the time, have become hereditary in cases where they did not exist. There were at all times non-official brehons, who were not attached to any clan and who held no land as a reward, but lived independently by their profession, and yet in these cases also the profession became hereditary.

Nor does the fact of having become hereditary appear to have led to the degradation and abuse which might be expected from it in our time, nor to have rendered the office of brehon more easily accessible than before. The essential standard of knowledge was in no degree lowered. The preparatory course of study continued to extend to twenty years. And of course the moral and other requirements were in no degree relaxed. Success as a brehon waited upon ability alone, and failure was attended by so many risks that the profession offered no attraction for unqualified persons. The brehons, like the old Saxon judges, but unlike modern judges, were always liable to damages, disgrace, and other grave punishments if their judgments were illegal or unjust.

The law says, "No person is qualified to plead a cause in the high court unless he is skilled in every department of legal science." There were several classes of advocates or pleaders, corresponding, perhaps, to Queen's Counsel and Barristers of the present day. There were, besides these, professional

lawyers of an inferior class somewhat analogous to
solicitors. It has been stated that one uniform
course of study was required, no matter what branch
of law a man intended to follow; that having gone
through that course he might become a brehon, an
ollamh, an advocate, or a law-agent, according to
his personal predilection, ability, and prospects of
practice. In my opinion, this is correct only *pro
tanto*. The course may have begun with the duties
of the law-agent, proceeding upward in succeeding
years until at the end of the brehon's term it included all branches of law, and it may have been
the same *so far as the other gentlemen pursued it ;* but
the brehon alone pursued it exhaustively, and
devoted twenty years of his life to that task. There
were, however, various distinctions between brehons
and advocates, and among the brehons themselves,
which are so difficult to follow that modern writers
are not at all agreed about them. In a society
wholly different from ours in its elements and construction those distinctions must have been made
on principles different from any now operating. It
does not follow that they were not proper distinctions. Our embarrassment is not necessarily due
to defect in those laws, but to our ignorance of them,
to our want of some missing link, perhaps many
missing links, in their consequential chain.

Each king, and each chief who was sufficiently
powerful, maintained a brehon, who was in a sense
the brehon of the territory. But the law did not
require this if there was an unofficial brehon in the

district.   The brehonship was rather a profession
than a state department.   The judicial institutions
were not strictly permanent with a regular order
of succession maintained systematically as men
dropped off, and wielding power given and sustained
by the state, as we now see.   When an official
brehon had died or ceased to act, unless there were
cases pending, or somebody sought his office with
the land that might have attached to it, there was
no immediate reason for appointing a successor; and
with regard to non-official brehons, when they were
removed by death or otherwise they can hardly be
said to have successors at all, or if so said it was
Nature supplied them in her own good time.   The
scope of a brehon's jurisdiction is not laid down in
the law, simply because no brehon had exclusive
jurisdiction anywhere, whether he was provided with
free land or not, whether his office had become hereditary or not.   The jurisdiction of official and of non-
official brehon alike was generally determined by
the suitors.   A defendant should consent to have
the case raised against him tried by *some* brehon,
or else judgment would go against him by default.
With this limitation the jurisdiction was purely consensual; the parties were free to settle their case
in private or to submit it to any brehon they pleased.
Of the brehons within reach, if more than one,
suitors displayed a preference for one beyond the
rest, and probably as a rule their choice was determined by his superior aptitude in unravelling knotty
problems and giving decisions consonant with justice.

Thus the brehon's position resembled that of an eminent Roman jurisprudens, whose opinion was eagerly sought and paid for by people in legal difficulties. He heard the case, gave it the necessary consideration, and pronounced a decision in accordance with law and justice. This decision, though called a judgment, and eminently entitled to that name, was not precisely what the word judgment means with us. It was rather a declaration of law and justice as applied to the facts before him, rather an award founded in each particular case on a submission to arbitration. There was no public officer whose duty is was to enforce the judgment when given. The successful party was left to execute it himself. In doing this he was assisted by the inherent equity of the particular judgment itself, by the force of an immemorial law universally obeyed, by public opinion informed by the generally prevalent love of justice, by the defendant's knowledge that delay, evasion, or resistance would be futile, would disgrace him and increase the penalty, and, above all, by that self-adjusting network of duties and obligations, involved in, and enforced by, the clan system. These combined forces went far to render executive officers of the law, as sheriffs, bailiffs, and police, unnecessary. They were practically irresistible, for they could go the length of outlawing a man and rendering his life and all he possessed worthless to him if he dared to withstand the execution of what a brehon had declared to be the demands of law and justice. They were

quite as effectual as is what we now call the arm of
the law, notwithstanding John Austin's theory, that
there can be no law except it be the command of a
sovereign.

There were certain cases which a brehon provided
with free land should hear and determine without
payment. Beyond these cases, the official brehon
and every other who tried a case were entitled to
be paid by the unsuccessful litigant certain fees,
which were fixed by the law according to the nature
of the cases, the trouble they entailed, and, in civil
cases, the amount of property involved. The amount
of the fee was a matter of calculation, according to
certain well-known rules, and it was always included
in the total amount to be paid under the judgment
by the unsuccessful party. In criminal cases one-
twelfth of the beaten party's honour-price was the
fee to be paid to the brehon. If the person charged
was found guilty he should pay this in addition to
any other fine imposed : if the accuser failed to
sustain his charge he had, if so sentenced, to pay
the judge in addition to compensating the accused,
and there was no occasion as now for a second trial.

When one brehon had adjudicated on a matter
submitted to him, there could be no appeal to
another brehon of the same rank ; but there might
be an appeal to a higher court, provided the
appellant gave security. The grounds of appeal
most frequently noticed are " sudden judgments,"
meaning probably those given without due consideration. If the facts of a case had undergone

a material change after trial and judgment, as if the defendant in a criminal case had been tried and fined for assault, and after the judgment the person assaulted had died, a new trial might be had.   In giving judgment in this second trial the judge would, of course, have regard to what was done under the first judgment.

Sub-Section 5.—The Ollamhs.

 CERTAIN writer boldly tells his readers that there were three class of judges, the Ollamh (pronounced *Ullav*) being the highest or chief judge. Most other authorities on the subject say that the brehons were judges, the ollamhs professors or teachers of law. The latter view is correct subject to the following obser- vations.   Every brehon was an ollamh, inasmuch as he was obliged to obtain the degree of ollamh before he could become a brehon.   Hence a man might practise as a brehon and teach law in his own house as an ollamh; and one who had dis- tinguished himself in both these respects might be regarded as, in a sense, a chief judge.   But the use of that designation is misleading.   Both ollamhs and brehons might as well be called bards on the ground that both were obliged to take a degree in poetry.   A loose application tends to involve those

terms in the confusion from which we have just
taken the trouble to extricate them.   Ollamh practically meant a doctor, professor, or teacher of any
branch of the Filidecht taught in the higher schools.
It meant a possessor of knowledge whose profession
it was to impart that knowledge. The right to the
distinction was acquired by a course of study extending over twelve years' " hard work," followed
by a public examination; and the distinction was
formally conferred by the king or chief of the district; after which the ollamh ranked next to the
king or chief in the order of precedence, acquired a
number of valuable privileges, was respected by the
community, and highly favoured by the law.   Every
king or chief who could afford it selected one distinguished ollamh of each branch of knowledge, and
maintained this staff of specialists at his court in
order to be able to deal with all matters affecting
his interests and those of his people.   These men
were very generously provided for, indeed extrava-
gantly one would think.   Other ollamhs made their
living by teaching independently.

Sub-Section 6.—*Jurors.*

BEFORE passing quite away from the legal system, a class of men, though not professional, connected with an important branch of the law may be noticed. They were drawn from the lay community in each *cinel* or *tuath*, and to twelve of them, as to a sort of jury, certain matters in dispute requiring knowledge other than legal were submitted, as, for instance, the manner in which land should be newly apportioned under the Irish system of gavelkind. The law determined the proportions, provided the quality of the land was uniform and other circumstances equal. As this would rarely happen in practice, these twelve men determined the actual proportions. They also arranged in the early part of each year how the common lands of each sept should be used that year. What the relations of those men to the clan were, what the qualification for the office, how the office descended, &c., are left open questions; and this is perhaps the best thing to do in the present neglected condition of the Brehon Laws. Still I should not be surprised if it were found on inquiry that it was not an office at all, but a power inherent in a certain status, and that every *flaith-fine*, or paterfamilias, was entitled to exercise it unless he had in some way forfeited his title.

SECTION IV.

THE FLAITHS.

LAITH may be pronounced *Flah*. The Flaiths corresponded in some respects to modern nobles, and like them originated in an official aristocracy. Theoretically they were public officers of their respective clans, each being at once the ruler and representative of a sept, were elected on the same principle as the kings, required similar qualifications according to rank, and were provided proportionately with free lands to enable them to support the dignity and perform the duties of the office. They also, like the kings, were allowed to hold at the same time all other property which they might have had or might subsequently inherit or otherwise acquire; and their position gave them some facilities of requisition which other men did not possess. Their official land was in law indivisible; an apparent

93

restriction which in practice became decidedly advantageous to them as a class, as we shall see.

The law gave the right of succession to the most worthy member of the *fine* of the actual flaith, subject to the right of the clan to determine by election what member of the *fine* was in fact the most worthy. Hence the flaith's successor might not be his son, though he had sons, but might be a brother, nephew, cousin, or other member of the *fine ;* and while the flaith's private property was on his death divisible among the members of his *fine* like that of any other individual, his official property with all the permanent structures thereon descended undivided to his successor, in addition to any share of the private property which might fall to that same person as a member of the *fine*. In course of time the hereditary principle encroached upon and choked the elective, the latter fell into desuetude, and the number of flaiths ceased to correspond to the number of septs. From the office and the land attached to it having been held successively by several succeeding generations of the same family, the flaith gradually learned to regard the land as his own private property, and the people gradually acquiesced ; and I find it laid down by a modern writer as the distinguishing mark 'of a flaith, that he paid no rent, and that a man who paid no rent was a flaith though he owned but a single acre. This writer completely lost sight of the fact that the flaith was properly an official, and the land he

held official land, and not his private property at all.
The system under which he lived, and of which he
formed a part, laid upon him certain duties for which
the lands and revenues assigned him were a provision and a reward, and it was only through the
decay and collapse of that system that he could
venture to call those lands and revenues his own.
The nature of his duties can most conveniently be
explained when discussing the next succeeding class
of society towards whom most of them were due and
owing; and there also it will become very obvious
that there was no such inadequate provision made
for a flaith as a single acre would have been.   It
will suffice to mention here that a very high private-
property qualification should have been possessed by
the family for three successive generations before one
could become a flaith at all; and then the official
property was given in addition to that.   In fact, the
flaiths were rather too well provided for, and were
so favourably circumstanced that ultimately they
almost supplanted the clan as owners of everything.

As the sea attracts all waters, as power and wealth
attract to themselves more power and more wealth,
the flaith class tended to become great at the expense of the people beneath them.   They were
constantly taking liberties with, and extending their
claims over, land to which they had no just title;
and the law under which official property descended
contributed to the same result.   The idea of private
property in land was developing and gathering

strength, and land was generally becoming settled
under it. The title of every holder, once temporary,
was hardening into ownership, and the old ownership of the clan was vanishing, becoming in ordinary
cases little more than a superior jurisdiction the
exercise of which was rarely invoked. During the
time of transition I think the flaith class encroached
upon the rights not alone of those below them but
of those above them also; that it was chiefly their
greed, pride, and disloyalty which led to the break-
up of the Irish Monarchy; and that it was for many
centuries in their power to restore that monarchy,
and with it an independent nationality, had they
been sufficiently patriotic.

The flaiths, by virtue of their office, had legal
jurisdiction in all matters coming under Urradhus
law, or law locally modified. There were various
grades or ranks among the flaiths as among modern
nobles, but determined by the number of clansmen
who paid them tribute; and the territorial limits of
a flaith's jurisdiction was wide or narrow as his rank
was high or low. When the legal system was in
proper working order, plaints involving Cāin law,
that is, the law contained in the Senchus Mōr and
administered by the brehons, were required to be
lodged at the residence of the Aire-ard before being
submitted to the brehons.

A great many varieties of *aires* are mentioned in
the laws; but generally the aire (pronounced *arra*)
appears to have been considered as the type of the
full citizen in possession of full legal rights. It was

a term not strictly applied, rather a measure of status which different classes might attain than the designation of any particular class. The flaiths and those approaching that rank were aires; and I think every head of a *fine* was in status an aire though not so called. The *aire* most frequently spoken of and the *aire-desa* were recent accessions to the flaith class from the Céile class, belonging by birth and descent to the latter, but possessing sufficient property qualification for the former; and, so far as there was progress, may be considered as in a state of transition. The *aire-desa* was the lowest of the flaith class. Part of his qualification was to have ten free clansmen paying tribute to him. The numbers paying tribute to the different grades of flaiths ranged from ten up to forty, the flaith's rank, honour-price, &c., ranging proportionately. The *bo-aire* was a man whose wealth consisted mainly in cattle. He was not a flaith.

8

SECTION V.

FREEMEN OWNING PROPERTY.

Sub-Section 1.—Preliminary.

N pursuance of our plan we now proceed to consider the free clansmen who held property. Property, for the most part, meant land, the cattle fed upon land, and the crops grown upon land. Our ancestors all lived in the country and mainly by industries connected with land. They had numerous villages, the earliest of which are indicated by the still existing raths; but they had few towns so large as to form distinct communities with life and interest different from those of the country. Our oldest maritime cities are of Danish origin. Hence the Brehon Laws are in the main applicable only to country life, and contain few rules specially applicable to town communities. The vast majority of freemen owning property were farmers, called Céiles, and for simplicity of description we will take this class as the standard.

The contemporary institutions of any given country are always so interwoven that it is difficult to discuss them separately, and impossible to give a complete account of one without giving as part of it some account of others connected with it. This is emphatically true of a country where society is organised on the system of *clan, sept,* and *fine.* That system is as soil in which all other institutions, like trees, have their roots. I have already had to anticipate myself in some respects. In order not to do so to a confusing extent, and in order to turn from hence on subsequent matters all the light we can, it will be necessary to deal, however briefly, with the clan system before treating specially of the Céiles, and to deal with the land system while discussing the Céiles.

Sub-Section 2.—*The Clan System.*

KNOWLEDGE of the real nature of the clan or tribal system would be a master-key to much connected with ancient Ireland that is now mysterious, and would remove many stumbling-blocks, if not all. Possibly the lost books, and lost portions of books, would have furnished this key and given us glimpses of life of which without them we can never dream. They would, at the very least, have illuminated some obscure passages in the existing remains which are now subjects of doubt and liable to misinterpretation. But without them full knowledge of this most interesting subject is lost to us, and if it be recoverable at all can only be so by the expenditure of much labour of many minds. For although the existing remains are in many parts extremely familiar with social and domestic economy, providing even for the legal enforcement of some duties which with us are of merely moral obligation, still the information given,

clear enough no doubt for those for whom it was intended, who knew its objects as self-evident facts and were themselves in the current of actual life, is in many respects not clear to us who grope in the dry channel through which that current passed. On certain points no information at all is given; and although great trouble is taken to explain other points, the writers, so to speak, do not begin at the beginning, but start on an assumed basis of knowledge which we no longer possess. We seek in vain for the why and the wherefore of things which apparently were so well known to the writers and their contemporaries that they did not need to be stated; and though much is said round and round a subject, the fundamental facts are evasive. From the time the system began to break up the prolonged agony of the nation has prevented the production of a writer capable of rescuing its fading features from oblivion. We are therefore obliged to pass over the subject very lightly and with uncertain tread, though it is really the most interesting branch, not alone of the law, but of the whole social and political economy. A few facts only appear to be pretty conclusively ascertained.

Mr. Seebohm, a diligent searcher after the truths of antiquity so far as regards England, comes to the conclusion that the tribal system was almost, perhaps wholly, universal—that is to say, that every nation has had its tribal period. He says, "It is confined to no race, to no continent, and to no quarter of the globe. Almost every people in

historic or prehistoric times has passed or is passing
through its stages." This is so ; but while in continental countries, owing to international friction
and other external influences, tribes generally
suffered disintregation and dissolution, and
ultimately disappeared, in Ireland, owing mainly
to its remoteness, insularity, and freedom from
those influences, the tribal system, while becoming
Hibernicised in some respects, perfected and
strengthened itself, and attained a highly artistic
degree of development such as it probably never
reached on any continent ; and it was made, and
long continued to be, the basis of right, duty,
property, law, and civilisation itself.

Tuath, *Cinel*, and *Clann*, were the words used
interchangeably to denote what we now call in-
differently a clan or tribe. It resembled the *Gens*
of ancient Rome in that all the members of it
claimed descent from a remote *fine*, and from a
common ancestor as head of that *fine*, and were
therefore kinsfolk, were entitled severally to various
rights dependent on the degree of relationship and
other facts, and formed collectively a state, political
and proprietorial, with a distinct municipal individuality and life, with a legislature of its own and
an army *in gremio;* but in these two latter respects
slightly subject to, and forming a member of, a
superior state consisting of a federation of similar
communities. Each clan was composed of a number
of septs, and each sept was composed of a number
of *fines*. Kinship was the web and bond of society

throughout the whole clan ; and all lesser rights whatsoever were subject to those of the clan. Theoretically it was a true kinship of blood, but in practice it may have been to some extent one of obsorption or adoption. Strangers settling in the district, conducting themselves well, and inter-marrying with the clan, were after a few generations indistinguishable from it. A chief or a flaith also occasionally wished to confer on a stranger the dignity and advantages of clanship—practically meaning citizenship—and when he had obtained the sanction of the clan assemblies, the stranger was adopted in the presence of the assembled clan by public proclamation. In the course of time the name *Tuath* came to be applied to the district occupied by a clan, and *Cinel* (pronounced *Kinnel*) was then the word used to denote the clan itself. *Fine* (pronounced *Finna*) was also sometimes used in the broad sense of clan, and this was not strictly incorrect since every clan originated in a small *fine;* but the word *fine* properly meant one of a number of sub-organisms of which the clan consisted. It was a miniature clan, and in fact the germ of a clan and the real social and legal unit. It was considerably more comprehensive than our word *family*. It has been compared with the Roman *familia*, but it was more comprehensive than even that. When complete it consisted of the *Flaith-fine* (also called *Ceann-fine*), and sixteen other male members, old members not ceasing to belong to it until sufficient new members had been born or adopted into it, upon which event

happening the old were in rotation thrust out to the
sept, and perhaps began to form new *fines*. Women,
children, and servants, did not enter into this com-
putation. The *flaith-fine*, or paterfamilias, was the
head and most important member of the group, in
some sense its guardian and protector, and was the
only member in full possession and free exercise of
all the rights of citizenship. All the members had
certain distinct and well-recognised rights, and, if of
full age, were *sui juris* and mutually liable to and for
each other; but so long as they remained in the *fine*,
the immediate exercise of some of their rights was
vested in the *flaith-fine*, who should act for them or
in whose name they should act. " No person who
is under protection is qualified to sue."

There are various conflicting theories as to the
persons of whom and the manner in which this
organism was composed, and even as to whether
it was in fact ever composed or ever existed except
as a legal fiction; and no explanation of it or conjecture about it is free from difficulty. Having
regard, however, to the frequent mention of it, and
of the " seventeen men " of whom it consisted, by
various legal and other writers at times far apart
and in various connections, it is quite impossible
to believe that it was fictitious; but in practice it
may not often have attained or long retained that
perfect organisation which the law contemplated;
and the law itself may have contemplated different
things at different times. Whether the members of
it became members on their birth, or on attaining

manhood and acquiring property ; whether they included or represented all within the ·fifth degree of relationship, or all within the seventeenth degree, are matters in dispute. Without presuming to settle them, let us construct a provisional *fine* for the purpose of conveying some idea of what it was like. When complete it consisted of " seventeen men " who were always classified in the following manner :—

1. The *Geilfine* consisted of the *flaith-fine* and his four sons or other nearest male relatives, most of whose rights were vested in him, who on his death were entitled to the largest share of his property, and would succeed to the largest portion of his responsibilities.

2. The *Deirbhfine* consisted of the four male members next to the foregoing in degree of relationship to the *flaith-fine*, upon whom, contingently, a smaller share of his property and responsibilities devolved.

3. The *Iarfine* consisted of the four males whose degree of relationship was still farther removed, and upon whom, contingently, still less property and responsibility devolved.

4. The *Innfine* consisted of four males the furthest removed from the *flaith-fine*, upon whom, contingently, the smallest portion of his property and responsibility devolved.

On the birth of a new male member in the first of these groups (or, according to a more probable theory, on his becoming a man and owner of ·property), the eldest member of that group was crushed out to the second group, the eldest member of the second group was crushed out to the third, the eldest member of the third was crushed out to the fourth, and the eldest member of the fourth, if he had not died, was crushed out of the *fine* altogether, and became an ordinary member of the *sept*, or clan, with no special rights or responsibilities in connection with his former *flaith-fine*. Thus the members of the groups were cast off like the coats of an onion, not all at once, but gradually, the groups themselves remaining complete all the time, and never exceeding four members each. And as they were cast off they suffered a loss of rights, but gained in freedom of action and freedom from liabilities, and the *flaith-fine* ceased to represent them, act for them, or be responsible for them. The members of the *fine* also owed a mutual responsibility to each other, were bound in certain cases to enter into suretiship for each other, were liable to compensate for crimes committed by any one of them if the criminal failed to do so; and in general the law held that there was a solidarity among them. A member who became a criminal was, of course, primarily liable for his own crimes. It would also appear that a person otherwise entitled to become a member in a certain event, forfeited that right, with all the advantages attached to it, by crime. My own opinion is that the members of the *fine* were all full-grown men living on divisions of a farm which had been originally one; yet that the group included only persons within the fifth or sixth degree of kindred, and did not extend to the seventeenth, and that the organisation was a natural outcome of the ordinary sentiment of family affection, perhaps somewhat intensified, but at all events systematised and enforced by law.

Various other *fines* are mentioned, and the word *fine* is used in a number of combinations; but the organism provisionally outlined is the only one of the name of real importance; and the text, after stating much about the seventeen men, adds, " It is then family relations cease." Presumably it was then the rights of inheritance and the dangers of liability also ceased.   Where in the system one should look for the exact counterpart of the modern family is not clear; nor is it clearly known whether the number of women, their presence or absence, at all affected the constitution of the *fine*.   The original purpose and main object of the whole system are, for lack of true knowledge, matters of much conjecture. It is probable that the system continued perfect only so long as the Celtic race remained pure and predominant, and that it became disorganised in the course of the thirteenth century.

The *Sept* was an intermediate organism between the *fine* and the clan.   It consisted of a number of *fines*, as the clan consisted of a number of *septs*.   It was one of the divisions of the clan assigned a specific part of the territory, and over it and this district a *flaith* was supposed to preside.   No rule is stated, and I think none existed, as to the number of persons or of *fines* that might be in a *sept*.   The right of the *sept* to undisturbed possession of its assigned portion of the territory was greater than that of the *fine*, was subject only to that of the clan, and was very rarely interfered with.

The rules of kinship by which the clan was formed were the same rules by which status was determined ; and this status in turn determined what a man's rights and obligations were, and largely supplied the place of contract and of laws affecting the disposition and devolution of property. The clan system aimed at creating and arranging definite rights and liabilities for every member of the clan at his birth, instead of leaving individuals to arrange these matters in their own ways. Kinship with the clan was the first qualification for the kingship, as for every minor office; and the king was the officer of the clan, and the type of its manhood, not its despot. Whatever its constitution, the clan when formed was a complete organic and legal entity or corporation, half social, half political, was proprietor of everything and supreme everywhere within its territory. Within historical times the clan owned the land —part of the land directly and immediately, the remainder ultimately. In earlier times it is very probable that the clan owned all the land and every other kind of property absolutely. It is very probable that at first neither individual property in land nor even the property of the *fine* in it was recognised, but only that of the clan, and that these smaller rights of property were at first temporary usufructs, which subsequently became permanent

encroachments on the rights of the clan. At no
time did the land belong either to the state in the
broad sense or to the individual absolutely. Each
clan was a distinct organism in itself, and the land
was its property—its absolute property at first, till
parts of it were encroached upon by the growth of
private rights, but its ultimate property so long as
the clan existed in its integrity. The clan was the
all-important thing. After the clan in degree of
importance came the *sept*, where one existed, and
then the *fine*. The individual was left little to do
but to fill the position assigned him and conform to
the system. Among ordinary people the *flaith-fine*
was the most important; but even his duties and
liabilities were so clearly laid down as part of the
system itself that he does not seem to have been left
a wide discretion. This insignificance of the individual seems to us calculated to stifle the best
qualities of man and to prevent all progress; and
the whole system seems to be one of disintegration
rather than of cohesion, and therefore adverse to the
growth and continued existence of a true state. Its
influence is so all-pervading in public as well as in
private life that it amounts to a different system of
civilisation from ours. The average young man from
Oxford or Cambridge, or even from Dublin Uni-
versity, with a mind full of fancy theories, may say
lightly that it is the absence of civilisation. It is
the absence of his civilisation, but not necessarily
of all. There existed a spiritual bond, purer and
more potent if wisely utilised than the modern one

of a common nationality, the creature of power.
And, however the fact is to be explained, the finest
qualities of our race have been exhibited under the
clan system. They may not have been due to it,
but it did not prevent them. Having regard to the
number of its inhabitants at the time, Ireland produced more distinguished men under the clan system
than it has since done. This is a fact which no
fancy theories can displace. It proves that, restricted though the clan system appears to us, it in
fact afforded sufficient margin for a person to distinguish himself. A large measure of individual
capacity was not alone attainable, but attained.
The bravest and most skilful warriors, the most
zealous and successful missionaries, poets, musicians, and literary men in astonishing numbers and
of astonishing power, taste, and skill, even some
artists whose works have scarcely ever been sur-
passed, and above all a virtuous and happy people,
grew up and flourished under the shadow, or the
light—whichever it was—of the clan system. All
this could not have been the absence of civilisation,
but really was a true civilisation different from ours.
Our modern notions are therefore an unreliable
standard by which to test or judge the clan system.
It is entitled, like every other system, to be judged
by its results. So judged it has produced much
which we are proud to inherit and might be proud
to produce. It is quite certain, too, that in those
far-off times the clan, with the rights it gave and
maintained, formed the greatest bulwark of the poor

and weak; and this explains to some extent the grateful tenacity with which the poor long clung to it. If it restricted men's natural right to make what bargains they pleased, the restriction applied most to the strong and wealthy; and if it arranged people's affairs for them to a large extent, the service was obviously most useful to those who, from any cause, were feeble. In this way it effectually prevented that violent antagonism of classes which is at once the danger and the disgrace of modern civilisation.

Sub-Section 3.—The Céiles and the Land Laws.

 TUATH, cinel, or clan occupied a given district, delimited by natural boundaries, as mountains and rivers, or by arbitrary boundaries first determined by the fortunes of war or otherwise. This whole district belonged, originally and ultimately, to the clan, as a corporation or community, and it was divided in the following manner for the benefit of that community:—Part was allotted to the king or chieftain, part to the flaiths and other public officers, part to the Céiles or free clansmen, for their respective homesteads, part called the Cumhal Senorba was placed under the control of the king or chieftain for the maintenance of the poor, old, and incapable members of the clan, and part called the Fearan Fine,

or tribe's quarter, was retained as the common
land of the whole clan, which every member of
the clan was free and equally entitled, *sub modo*,
to use. None of this last was held as private
property, except for one year, at the end of
which it would become common again. There
was also a portion of land, the extent of which
was diminishing with the progress of ages, which
occupied an intermediate position between the
private land and the common land in this, that,
on the death of a holder, all the land of this class
held by his sept was divided anew. The land, as
regards quality, generally ranged in the order set
out, beginning with the king's best, which was
usually that longest in cultivation, and ending with
the common waste. The land held in common,
however, was not all bad land or waste; some of
it was cultivated and some meadowed. Land
holders may be divided into three general classes,
namely; first, all who held land officially, including
the king, the professional men, and the flaiths;
second, the Céiles, or ordinary free clansmen, who
held land (as one may say) by birthright, who were
the bone and muscle of the community, paid fixed
tributes for the maintenance of the state, and formed
its army in time of war; third, the non-free people,
some of whom held land under contracts.

It is said by one recent writer that the Céiles were
freemen who placed themselves under the protection of a flaith; and another likens them to the
Roman *Clientes*, which is substantially the same

CLASSIFICATION OF SOCIETY. 113

thing. I believe this to be a direct inversion of
what they were. They were the ordinary free
clansmen, who, as such, held land by as good a
title as then existed, by as good a title as that
of the flaith himself. Their rights, to their proper
extent, originated in the law like his, and were as
fully secured by the law as his. Instead of placing
themselves under the protection of a flaith in the
sense suggested, they placed, or at all events had
the right to place, a flaith of their own choosing
and of their own kindred over them to represent
them and act for them as occasion required, and
to protect, not appropriate, their rights. The two
views may practically amount to the same thing if
the period viewed is that of the clan's decay; but
one is offensive and repugnant to an efficient clan
system, while the other harmonises with that system
and is not offensive.

Another modern writer says that the power of
disposing of one's own several property was unlimited. He does not state his authority; nor
what he means by property; nor whether he means
property in land or property in chattels. The power
of disposing of property in chattels has in all ages
and countries been freer than the power of disposing of land. Property in ancient Ireland appears
to have been divided into, not real and personal,
but separable and inseparable. The inseparable
included all lands and a great deal of chattels, and
the separable the remainder of the chattels; and
although this division may not have been made

9

specially with reference to the right of disposal,
it is pretty safe to assume that that right coincided
with it.   In many parts of the law, in both text
and commentary, there is clear evidence that the
individual had not an absolute and unfettered right
of entering into important contracts of any kind
without the concurrence of others. That being so
he could not have an absolute right to sell, which
is one of the most important forms of contract at
the same time that it is in general an exercise of
the right of personal ownership. If by absolute
ownership is meant unlimited and perpetual power
of use and disposal, then no such thing as absolute
ownership of land existed; and the person called
owner was but _part owner, part agent, and part
trustee for life, with right of enjoyment. The *fine*
or sept occupied the position of principal and *cestui
que trust.* With the concurrence of the *fine* or sept,
the individual could confer an almost absolute title.
Without this concurrence he could not. Though
the céiles owned, in a sense, the land about their
homesteads, and no doubt called it their own, they
certainly had not an absolute right either during
life or at death to dispose of it to a person outside
the clan. Tenure depended on, and was subject to,
the tribal status not of the immediate holder alone,
but of other members of the *fine*, who had in the
property vested rights of a character and extent
defined by the law. Neither the land nor the tenure
of it belonged exclusively to the individual, but
partly to the *fine*, contingently to the sept—a wider

circle ; and though all these had waived or forfeited their rights, or had died, the holder did not thereby acquire a right of absolute disposal, for the paramount rights of the clan itself intervened. And apart from these considerations, and its general repugnancy to the clan organisation, a right of absolute disposal is expressly negatived by distinct passages in the law.   In the Corus Bescna we read, " No person should grant land except such as he himself has purchased, unless by the common consent of the tribe, and that he leaves his share of the common lands to revert to the common possession of the tribe after him." That is a perfectly clear statement.   Again we read, " It is one of the duties of the tribe to support every tribesman, and the tribe does this when in its proper condition.   The proper duties of one towards his tribe are, *that when he has not bought he should not sell;* that he does not wound ; nor desire to wound or betray." From these two passages it is quite clear that the sale of inherited land was not absolutely free.   It by no means follows that the sale of purchased land was wholly free from restriction. Little land was purchased, and clearly the sale of it was freer than the sale of inherited land.   Even on the disposal of chattels, such as cattle, there were some restrictions.   An owner about to sell them should inform the flaith or chief of his tuath of his intention ; and the chief or flaith or any member of the tuath who required the thing about to be sold had a right of pre-emption or first offer.

The ownership of the clan, at first real and positive
enough, was becoming vague, indefinite, and scarcely
conscious or operative except when the need or the
interest of the clan or of a member of the clan was
shown to call for its exercise.   This most frequently
existed and could most easily be shown in connection with land, the most valuable of all property ;
but it might also be occasionally shown in a
sufficiently acute form if an owner of cattle drove
them away and sold them to strangers, while the
lands of the clan were understocked.   And among
small farmers who were often joined for purposes
of ploughing, to allow one of such partners to sell
his draft beasts at a particular time when his own
work was done but not that of his partner, would
be to allow injustice ; and the laws preferred
prevention to punishment.

In connection with this question of disposal, it
may not be amiss to point out in passing that in
many countries in ancient times property in land
was transferred only in a court of law, and that
in England the alienation of land was not free until
two centuries after the Norman Conquest.

The land held by the céiles as private property,
and on which they resided, was subject to an annual
ciss (=tribute), rather in the nature of revenue for
clan purposes than of rent, and to smaller payments
resembling rates.   All tributes were paid in kind,
and wealthy people had to pay in reflections also—
which, of course, was a species of payment in kind.
Money was little known or used.   There is no

mention of it in the Senchus Mōr. It is mentioned
a couple of times in the commentaries on other
law tracts. Articles of gold, silver, and copper are
spoken of; but not money in the text. An article
called a *sicail* is spoken of in the commentary.
Although it was of a fixed value, I think from its
having been used only by ladies that it was considered rather an ornament than a coin. Ordinary
céiles paid in horses, cattle, sheep, goats, pigs, and
other animals, alive or dead; wheat, barley, malt,
flax, onions, dye-plants, firkins of butter, meal, wool,
honey, and other products of the land, with, in
most cases, "a handful of candles eight fists in
length." These candles were partially peeled
rushes dipped in fat. Bees and honey are so
frequently mentioned in the laws that the editors
remark that from the Brehon Laws alone a code
on the subject of bees might easily be gathered.
A curious code it would be too. An owner of bees
was obliged to distribute every third year a portion
of his honey among his neighbours, because the
bees had gathered the honey off the neighbours'
lands. There is even a special tract on "Bee
Judgments." The importance of bees was largely
due to the fact that sugar was unknown. Honey
was probably the only sweetening material in use.
It was used also in the manufacture of mead; and
beeswax was used in the manufacture of candles,
chiefly those employed at royal entertainments and
as altar lights. In such times bees with their
honey and wax constituted a valuable property.

The ancient laws of Wales also contain many
rules relating to bees and honey, far more than
the present importance of these things would
justify.

Craftsmen and others who could make useful or
ornamental articles, and who at the same time held
some land, paid for it by whatever they could make,
as machinery, agricultural and household implements,
tools of various kinds, furniture, articles of clothing,
bedding, linen, swords, shields, musical instruments,
ornaments of various kinds for the person and for
the home; in short, whatever the skill of one could
produce and the fancy of another desire. Manu-
factured articles being then of greater value than
now, and land being cheaper, those articles would
pay for more land. Some persons also held land,
as in England and on the Continent, by services—
services against wolves, pirates, and other enemies;
but this species of tenure does not appear to have
been either extensive or continual. There was no
such thing as tenure by ordinary military service. It
was at once the right and the duty of every free
clansman to render this, whether he held land or
not; and a person who, in the absence of sickness or
other valid excuse, failed to render military service
when required suffered a reduction of status—a
diminution of rights and powers. Cottiers holding
small plots of land immediately from the flaith often
paid for it in manual labour.

In respect of the quantities of the things paid in
kind, nice calculations must have been difficult,

but the laws distinguish three degrees. The first and lowest was the *ciss* fixed by law as payable by every clansman who held land. In the English version of the *Ancient Laws of Ireland* this word is translated " rent." This is due to the modern importance of rent acting on the minds of the translators. Rent is neither a correct translation of the word nor a correct description of the thing. The correct translation of *ciss* is *tribute ;* and the *ciss* was not rent, but tribute. It constituted the ordinary revenue for public purposes ; and it was levied on land as being at once the principal class of property and the natural source of support for the state. The second species of payment resembled rent more closely, being a stipulated payment for land to which a man had no title arising from clan status or from the law. The third was called the *ciss ninscis*, or *wearisome tribute*, and it was rent in reality. It was paid under agreement by a person who did not belong to the clan, that is, either by an outsider or a non-free person residing in the territory.

The measures by which the actual quantities in each case were ascertained were the *cumhal* (pronounced *cooal*) and the *sed* (pronounced *shed*). These terms are of constant recurrence throughout the laws wherever measurable quantities are in question. Cumhal means, literally, a bond-maid or female slave; but in the laws it is never used in any other sense than as a measure of quantity, or rather of value, perhaps what was originally supposed to equal the value of such a slave. As applied to land (*tir-cumhal*), it meant the usufruct for one year of about twenty acres, less or more, according as the land was good or bad. For land was not always measured by its actual superficial extent, but by the number of cows it was capable of feeding. This is still quite a usual mode of measuring land and of calculating its worth. Also if a mill or other useful or profitable structure stood on the land, less of that land would amount to a cumhal than if there were no such structure. In short, cumhal was a measure of value, not of extent. As applied to other things than land, cumhal meant the value of three cows. Translators appear to hesitate at the word *sed*, probably on account of the number of senses in which it is used. It is rendered, " a jewel, a cow, a thing of value." It, however, does not mean any particular species of property, but a certain standard of value, irrespective of species ; and in the Senchus Mōr five seds equal three cows. Of course the knowledge of these equivalents hardly helps us at all in determining the present money value of either.

The free clansmen had, in addition to their private lands, the right to turn out cattle and swine to graze on the Fearan Fine or common land, the number of beasts that each person might so turn out being fixed in a general way by the law and specifically determined by the jury already mentioned. This use was not free, however. The rent usually paid for it was one animal yearly for every seven fed in this way.

A céile who required more land than he possessed
could obtain it from the chief for one year, or, with
the consent of the tribe, permanently, out of the
Fearan Fine or any waste land that could be spared.
For this the céile paid tribute of the second class
mentioned above for ten years, after which the land
was subject only to tribute of the first class. The
land having in the meantime become more valuable,
it is possible that the actual amount of the tribute
remained the same.

Of the smaller payments to which landholders
were subject, some were certain, others contingent.
One of the certain payments was that made by all
for the support of the poor, the aged, orphans, and
the like belonging to the clan, in addition to the
Cumhal Senorba, or Old Age Inheritance, which
stood dedicated to their use. The immediate relatives of a criminal were contingently liable to pay
compensation for his misdeeds ; and the sept, and
even the whole clan, were liable in the contingency
of the nearer relatives failing. There was also a
somewhat similar liability in respect of certain
contracts, if entered into with the consent of the
relatives or of the clan.

All the tributes mentioned were paid to the flaith,
not as landlord but as a public officer, not for his
own use, except so far as the absence of money and
other circumstances rendered his use necessary, but
to be spent in the interests of the clan. Neither the
land nor the tribute issuing out of it belonged to the
flaith. He had no power whatever to evict a clans-

man, *whether the tribute was paid or not.* He might
evict an outsider, or a non-free person, to whom he
had let land by agreement, if the rent agreed upon
was not paid, or for other sufficient cause. But the
free clansman's tenure was not the result of any
agreement, and was not from the flaith at all, but
was a right accruing to him at his birth; and if he
was in default with the tribute the utmost the flaith
could do against him was to distrain his cattle or
other goods for the amount due. In the case of a
number of debts due by the same person, and sued
for at the same time, arrears of tribute had to be
paid first; but if a céile died owing arrears of tribute,
the amount of those arrears could not be recovered
from the céile's heirs. "Every dead man kills his
liabilities. It results from the neglect of the flaith
that there is no liability upon the heirs of the céile,
unless they themselves have committed default after
the death of their father."

The collection and expenditure of tribute was the
weakest point in the whole Irish system, as it was
in that of Rome. The Roman system of government was probably as perfect for the time as is any
system of modern Europe, with the exception of
this one flaw—the taxes were farmed out to under-
takers to collect, instead of being collected by the
State. The Irish system provided the flaith for the
collection of the tributes, but left them when collected in the hands of the collector. The flaith was
at once state receiver and chief executive officer of
his district. What did he do with all this rent in

kind which was being continually heaped upon him? The system theoretically provided many useful things for him to do with it ; but the temptation to abuse his position gained as that system lost in controlling power. He was obliged to pay some tribute to the king or chief above him. In time of war he was bound to provide a fixed number of men and horses, together with food for them. He was bound to entertain the king and certain high officials with their respective retinues on certain periodic visits. He was bound to make suitable provision for the public officers of his own small territory. He was bound, with the concurrence of the local assemblies, to keep roads, bridges, and ferries in repair and to make new ones where necessary ; to provide protection against storms and floods ; to maintain the public mill of the district, the public fishing-net, and other public institutions which varied with the nature of the district. It was his duty to supply, where needful, the · farmers and cottiers with live stock for their lands, chiefly young cattle, according to their various wants, the quality of the land they held, and other circumstances, so that they might, by feeding and using these animals in their respective ways, support themselves and pay the tribute out of the profits. One farmer would, from taste or suitability of circumstances, make a specialty of breeding one particular class of stock, another a different class ; and the flaith took up the tributes from the different men at different seasons of the year, thus making the supply keep pace with the demand, always having enough on hands to satisfy all requirements, and letting out to one what he had received from another.   In order that the supply should not fail and that the sept should not suffer, the law required every clansman who had a super-fluity of stock to dispose of to apprise the flaith of his district before selling them, and the flaith was empowered to enforce this law if necessary.   The flaith was also bound to provide bulls and stallions for the use of the sept.   These were very useful functions, and they by no means exhausted the duties which by law the flaith was bound to dis-charge, and probably did discharge (through ser-vants, of course), so long as the local assemblies exercised their powers of guidance and control.   The tributes being in kind, too, it really was hard to make a better use of them than that indicated. But the system was a bad one, bound to break down as soon as the check of a local assembly was removed.   Perhaps the flaith exacted nearly as much tribute from the people in a time of peace as in a time of war, and perhaps after exacting tribute he left public works undone, or left those who had paid for them to do them as well; and with so much property of various kinds in his hands and coming into them, and a feeble assembly or none to demand it or an account of it from him, the temptation to regard it all as his own imposed a strain on the virtue of the flaith, impelling him at once to oppress those beneath him and to shirk his own duty to those above him and to the State.   The state receiver became a receiver for himself; the executive officer did not trouble himself to execute much beyond what was to his own advantage.

Some landholders of adequate means raised sufficient stock for their own use, and had no occasion to purchase or hire stock; or they purchased what they wanted in the ordinary way, from the flaith or from somebody else, and had no account to render. All the Céiles were classified as *Saer* and *Daer*, which terms are translated as *free* and *base* respectively. We are told that the difference was like that which prevailed, and to some extent still prevails, in England between freeholders and copyholders. Beyond this vague comparison, those who make it do not attempt to explain the distinction in the case of those who did not hire stock; and if the distinction existed among such céiles—as it appears to have done—I have failed to discover in what it consisted. Of this I am very sure, that the difference was *not* the same as that between English freeholders and copyholders, that the conditions of the one country rendered the relations of the other wholly inapplicable, and that the references made to those tenures do not help us in the least. Possibly they are as often made to excuse the writer from explaining as to assist readers to understand. In my opinion, the tenure of all who did not hire stock was a perfectly free tenure, and in their case the terms saer and daer had reference to their comparative wealth and status, and not to the nature of their tenure.

The transactions of the flaith in cattle, however,

appear to have consisted in practice mainly in letting
out cattle on what may be called a hire-purchase
system, which itself was of two kinds; and it is in
the difference between these two kinds that, so far
as regards the céiles who hired stock, the real difference between saer and daer consisted. The translators describe this difference, in half-English, as
saer-stock tenure and daer-stock tenure. One of our
modern writers says that the difference between the
saer-stock and the daer-stock tenant was, that the
latter paid *Biathad* (pronounced *Beeha*), a word
signifying *Food-Tribute*, or a payment made in any
eatable material. This is a mistake. Nominally,
indeed, certain persons were bound to pay certain
amounts of food-tribute, but in practice either or
both paid it whenever it happened to be the most
convenient form of payment. It was in the *quantity*
and the other terms that the difference consisted.
And with regard to both these terms, *tenure* being a
word used in English law only with reference to land
or something issuing out of land, it can hardly be a
correct translation at all, since what the flaith let
out to the céiles was not land but cattle. In what
is called saer-stock tenure the flaith gave the stock
without requiring any security, and without any
bargain whatever, but subject to the general law
which was known to both parties. My own impression is that the flaith was bound to do this, and that
the person to whom he so gave stock was a clansman
entitled to get stock in this way, and was not a
tenant at all. However, let that pass. The flaith

gave the stock, and for it the law entitled him to an annual return for seven years of one-third the value of the stock given. This payment being duly made, at the end of seven years the stock became the absolute property of the céile, and he had no more to pay for them. This was a substantial return. Though not so heavy as modern rent, especially in view of its short duration, it was heavier than the gross amount of tributes paid by the céiles who did not hire stock. The céile might, if he liked, not begin to pay the instalments until the end of the third year, but he was bound to pay up then for those three years.

Daer-stock tenure, among those who hired cattle, was somewhat similar ; but the tenant had to give security for the stock, to render a larger return than the saer-stock tenant did, and if he was a free clansman entitled to take saer-stock the fact of his taking daer-stock seriously affected his status and that of his *fine*, rendered him incompetent to give evidence in a court of justice in opposition to the evidence of a flaith, and diminished or extinguished his right, and the right of his *fine*, to recover eric or other fine in the event of injury done to him or them. These were such grave consequences that a free clansman could not take daer-stock without the consent of his *fine*, and it was only the pressure of poverty would induce him to take daer-stock at all. War generally reduced large numbers to this necessity. It is probable that the law originally contemplated the taking of daer-stock only by men who were not true clansmen.

The rights and duties of both parties in these transactions are so fully and minutely laid down in the laws that there was little occasion for specific contracts, and probably business was done as smoothly without them as with them. There was more need of specific contract in base tenure than in the other, since, although it was provided for by the law, it originated not in a birthright like the other tenure, but in an agreement express or implied. Neither of the tenures was liable to capricious determination by either party. But for just and sufficient cause, and subject to fair conditions, either party might bring the arrangement to an end. It is said that the daer-céile as well as the saer-céile was able, for just cause, to have the contract set aside; but it is not clear how he could do this except with the voluntary consent of the flaith, first, because the flaith held security, and secondly, because the daer-stock tenant was incompetent to give evidence against a flaith.

If a céile who had taken stock absconded without paying the value, and left no property behind him but the land, unless the *fine* paid for the cattle the flaith was entitled to take and hold so much of the land as would compensate him. The remainder went to the *fine* of the absconding debtor, subject to any debts due by him.

In the laws a daer-man or daer-person is mentioned as distinct from a daer-stock tenant, and " the full eric fine of a daer-man " is frequently spoken of. What exactly this person was I cannot ascertain.

Sub-Section 4.—Devolution of Property.

NITY of ownership in the clan, so long as it existed and so far as it extended, prevented the devolution of property to individuals in the same sense as in English law. Even to a late period a considerable portion of land was not inheritable by individuals, but remained unchangeably the property of the clan as an immortal corporation. To this land, therefore, no rules of devolution applied. Orba, or lands of inheritance, descended in three different ways :—

1. *According to the rules of gavelkind.* I place this first, not because it was the most important in historical times, but because it was the oldest, was once general, and certainly was the most unlike anything we are now acquainted with. Land held by a man outside his home farm, and which occupied an intermediate position between his private land and the common land of the clan, descended according to the Irish system of gavelkind, that is, on the holder's death not only the particular land

10

which had been thus held by him, but all the land of
the same class belonging to his *sept*, was divided
anew amongst the adult males of the sept.   It was
an unsettled system.   Still it must be admitted that
it gave some start in life, however crude, to young
men who might otherwise have got none.   On such
a division of land, the amount of it that each person
was entitled to receive was fixed in general theory
by the law, subject to adjustment in each particular
case by a court of twelve men who took differences
of quality and other relevant facts into consideration.
Their decisions do not appear to have been questioned.   If they ever were questioned, no doubt an
appeal lay to the brehons.   Under this peculiar
custom of descent women appear to have been ex-
cluded. The amount of land subject to the custom constantly diminished, the custom receding, as it were,
from good land and extending to land little cultivated.
I think the land subject to this custom must have
been unfenced, but it is not so stated.   It was that
portion of the land of the sept over which an individual right of private property had not yet attained
maturity, the interest of each holder not being
ownership nor quite a life interest.   A large proportion of the good land of Ireland must have been
rescued from this custom a century or two before
the birth of Christ, if it be true as stated that large
quantities of corn were grown and exported in those
centuries to Britain, Gaul, and Spain, a thing hardly
possible if the land had remained unfenced and subject to this unsettled species of gavelkind.   At the

time of Cæsar's arrival in Britain the land there was
wholly unfenced, except the mounds and fallen
timber that encircled the fortresses and clustering
hamlets. There was no division into fields, the land
being distinguished only as cleared and uncleared in
respect of forest, and the people subsisting mainly on
meat and milk. But Ireland was more advanced at
that time, and (or perhaps *because*) it was more
accessible to and more frequented by merchants
from the then enlightened nations of the world, the
state of Northern Europe being such that merchants
could not cross overland in safety. Some of the
good land of Ireland was fenced at a very early date,
and the law affecting fences and mearings is old and
and yet elaborate. The nature of the fence affected
the liability for trespass upon land; hence in dealing
with that subject the law describes the fences. There
were ditch-and-mound fences, wall fences, stake
fences woven with rods and having a blackthorn
crest on the top; and some others.

2. *As private property.* In this case, on the death
of the father of a family each member of his *Geilfine*
—usually meaning each son not already provided for
—was entitled to an equal share of the land and of
the cattle fed upon it; but one of the sons, in
addition to his equal share, inherited all the houses
and offices constituting the homestead, the valuable
fixtures which usually stood upon the same land, and
the household, farming and manufacturing implements. Whether this favoured son was the eldest or
the youngest is one of the disputed points in connec-

tion with that obscure subject the organisation of
the *fine*. The preponderance of opinion at present
seems to be in favour of the eldest son, and this is
probably correct as applied to the Middle Ages ; but
I incline to the belief that earlier it was the youngest
son who was so favoured. However this may be, as
a counterpoise and consideration for the special
inheritance, the law held him responsible, as
succeeding *flaith-fine* and stem of the family, for the
guardianship of his sisters until their. marriage and
of any other dependent members of his *fine*, obliged
him to act as plaintiff and defendant as became
necessary in all suits at law concerning them or their
property ; and if he was of proper grade bound him
to entertain the king, bishop, bards, brehons, and
others with their respective retinues. In the foregoing circumstances all the land went to the sons,
and daughters had either to depend on the husbands
they got or to be provided for out of the movable
property. On the occasion of almost every marriage
there was a collection, called a *Tinol*, made among
the relatives and given to the bride. But this can
hardly have been a very substantial amount, and it
probably corresponded to modern wedding presents.
If daughters were more numerous than sons, and
could not be provided for out of the movable
property without gross inequality, one or more of
their husbands might be admitted to an equal share
of the land, and then questions of status would arise
as to which of them this should be. If there were
no sons, the land, anciently, went to the nearest

male members of the *fine* in the order already described, subject to a provision being made out of it for the daughters. The exclusion of daughters from inheritance seems to us very unfair; but it was no more so then in Ireland than it was many centuries later under the Normans in England. The chief reason for it in the latter case was, that the land was held by military service, which women were incapable of rendering. The Irish got rid of the anomaly long before the introduction of Christianity, through the exertions, it is said, of Brīg Ambui. She is described by some as a lady judge. There were no lady judges. She was the wife of a judge, made use of her position to acquire an exceptional knowledge of law, gave advice to women regarding the taking possession of land which they claimed, and her advice was so skilful that she succeeded in winning, not alone their particular cases for her clients, but legal equality for her sex in general. She was probably assisted by two facts, namely, that military tenures in the Norman sense did not exist in Ireland, and that Irish women were in those times free and liable to bear arms. However it came about, in the Middle Ages in Ireland, if there were no sons the property was divided equally among the daughters. With regard to the further descent of land thus given to daughters, the text says, "As to a mother's land, her sons shall divide it from the days of her public testament. But the half of it shall revert to the tribe of the original owner of the land; the other half according to true judgments the seed of her flesh divide."

3. *According to the rules of tanistry.* In order to secure to kings, chiefs, flaiths, and other public officers who acted on behalf of the community, their ancient affluence permanent and undiminished, with all its attendant advantages, the law held the lands assigned them for their public services to be indivisible. The land held by each descended to his successor, as the property of a corporation does in English law. The successor was usually a near relative, but not necessarily so. Thus while the lands held by ordinary people underwent repeated subdivision as they descended, and the rights and privileges which landed property conferred were similarly subdivided, constantly tending downwards to small patches, few rights, and little power, a position of permanent and disproportionate wealth with its attendant power was secured to the people of rank; and what was apparently a restriction, and was originally intended as such, became in operation a class privilege. And although the flaiths had practically appropriated the official lands to their own families, so far from desiring to free those lands from this rule of descent, they maintained the rule and even extended it to all the lands they could in any way acquire.

RETURNING to the subject of tenure; in describing the céiles I have endeavoured to give a general outline of the element in which they lived, namely, the law affecting property in land. That law was as unlike the system called Feudalism as any that ever existed; so unlike, indeed, that it has been called, and truly, called, the very antithesis of feudalism. This being so, it is strange and confusing to find Irish scholars of the present day writing and speaking of Irish feudalism, and representing the ghastly struggle of Queen Elizabeth's reign as one between Irish feudalism and English anti-feudalism; the real fact being that there has never been such a thing as Irish feudalism. The feudal system of land tenure prevailed for several centuries over England, Scotland, and a large portion of the continent of Europe, and it is still distinctly traceable in

the laws of those countries; so much so that a
thorough knowledge of real property law at the
present day cannot be acquired until one has first
made himself acquainted with the leading features of
the feudal system. Those features do not exist in
the system I have just outlined. Feudalism never
prevailed in Ireland, never existed there, and the
system that did prevail was as unlike feudalism as
could well be devised. The relation between the
flaith and the céile was not one of tenure at all in
the proper meaning of that word. The nature of
that relation is wholly misconceived by any one who
looks for tenure in it. A tenure did exist, as we
shall see; but it existed between the flaith and the
non-free people, not between the flaith and the
clansmen. The land belonged neither to the king
nor to a lord, but to the clan, including high and
low. What the flaith held, what the céile held, and
what neither held, belonged alike to the clan. And
even when a clansman sought and obtained more
land than his status entitled him to, and a relation
resembling tenure arose respecting this land, that
relation was not with the flaith, except as the official
through whose instrumentality it was contracted,
but with the clan of which the céile and the flaith
were alike members. The feudal principle of
primogeniture was not recognised by the law in
regard to either rank or property. Instead of it, and
in contrast with it, the law provided for *election* to
every office, with the addition that the most worthy
should be elected, and provided that property should

descend to those who had the strongest natural
claim, in shares which were in effect proportioned to
the strength of that claim. It is surely a strange
mistake to call such a system feudalism. As
Professor O'Curry says, "Feudal land laws never
prevailed in any form in ancient Erinn."

One element resembling feudalism ran through
the whole Irish system from the king to the
humblest person who paid tribute. This was the
custom according to which when any one, high or
low, paid tribute he was always given something in
return by the person to whom he had just made the
payment. Precisely the same rule was observed on
the payment of tribute by the chief of a tuath to a
provincial king, and on the payment of tribute by the
provincial king to the Ard-Rīg. The thing given in
return was usually something of little value, but the
acceptance of it is interpreted by writers of the
present day, arguing from the heriot of English
copyhold tenure, to have been the acceptance of a
position of vassalage. Personally, I believe this to
be a purely gratuitous assumption based upon a false
analogy. This single ceremony, even if it were
shown to have had any relation to land, cannot
neutralise every other fact connected with the holding of land. It is at least as likely to have been a
recognition of allegiance as a yoke of tenure. What
its real meaning was, since it cannot yet be determined with certainty, had better be left in honest
doubt until through further research certainty
is reached. In the light of our present defective

knowledge, the custom appears inconsistent with the clan organisation, and yet it seems to have prevailed when that organisation was in vigour ; and it certainly was entirely native and not derived from the feudalism of England or the Continent.

It is true that the Irish system was undergoing a change amounting to decay, and was drifting in the direction of feudalism at the time that feudalism was dying out in England. Various causes, political, social, and economic, contributed to this. First of all, the radical defect in the system itself in regard to the collection and disbursement of the tributes. Then of historical causes, chiefly contact and friction with non-Celtic elements, beginning with the wars with the Danes, which deranged the mechanism and disturbed the smooth operation of the Gaelic system. Before the country had recovered from the disorder thus occasioned, the Anglo-Normans arrived, prevented recovery, and contributed to the progress of decay in the following, among other ways. While as a rule adopting the Brehon Laws, so far as their personal interests were served by doing so—adopting the advantages without the correlative restraints and responsibilities — those settlers introduced to the districts grabbed by them a few of the rules of feudalism and some of the feudal spirit. Emboldened by the force of this example, and by avarice, some of the flaiths who were the Gaelic neighbours of those settlers, and who had long been treating as their own property that which was originally official, at times of disorder and consequent relaxation of the Gaelic discipline, extended their pretensions, began to assert their personal individuality over that of the community, to regard themselves as lords in the feudal sense, to treat the tributes paid to them, and even the lands out of which those tributes issued, as in some sense their own, and to treat as tenants men who had hitherto been their fellow clansmen. The presence of two rival races in the land, and the consequent frequency of war, afforded occasions sufficiently numerous for the progress of this constitutional gangrene. Favoured by these circumstances, and prompted by self-interest, Gaelic flaith and Norman settler alike developed a strong personality, acquired undue prominence as military leaders, prevented the regular meetings of the local assemblies, marred and paralysed them when they did meet, rendered the formation of effective public opinion impossible in any way, and reduced the former clansmen or their descendants to the position of mere retainers. True progress there could be none, and as nations seldom stand still there was a retrograde movement. The old temporary tributes here and there degenerated into permanent rents; the old tenure of cattle into a tenure of the land upon which the cattle were fed; clan rights became more and more vague, the personal rights of people of rank more and more accentuated, the personal rights of humble people less so. The situation became altogether favourable for the introduction of feudalism, but it was never introduced; for the evolution of a native feudalism,

but it was never evolved. For, after all, this retro-
gression was comparatively late and trifling, and as
a fact it never found its way into the laws at all, but
was constantly localised and counteracted by the
laws as a disease. It was quite alien to the laws ;
and, so far as it did extend, represented not Irish
laws but the violation of them. Those laws continued to be the laws of the whole country except
the Pale until the beginning of the seventeenth
century ; and long after their formal abolition under
James the First, the people clung to them—as well
they might—as tenaciously as they could; and the
peasantry down to the present day have, in the face
of stern laws, clung to the old Gaelic idea that the
land belongs to the people, an idea wholly irreconcilable with feudalism.

The change in the land laws was one of the most
important legal changes made by the English in
Ireland. Without touching upon the question
whether it was or was not necessary, it certainly
could have been effected either without injustice
to anybody or with very cruel injustice to the mass
of the people. The latter was the method pursued.
The Anglo-Norman settlers from the very beginning
recognised and respected the rights conferred by
tribal status. Indeed, it was impossible to do otherwise in a country where all rights were so conferred.
To do otherwise would have been universal robbery,
and this they were neither able nor inclined to carry
out. But English rulers, from the Tudor period
downwards, refused to recognise any such rights

in the people, and, when it suited their purpose, conferred upon chiefs and flaiths rights which the clan system never gave them. Though a man was in the actual possession of land descended to him in strict accordance with immemorial custom, if he was unable to show a record, or a contract on parchment duly sealed and delivered, he was treated as a mere tenant at will or a trespasser, and his land was given to an Englishman who had neither tribal nor any other right whatsoever. The Irish in general had, of course, no such muniments of title to show. They held their lands as their ancestors had held them, by right of birth in the clan. This meant to the English mind no right at all. Its assertion was rather an outrage. The general absence of contract was made a pretext for general confiscation. This, so far as relates to land law, was the real nature of the struggle that was in progress during the Tudor period, was atrociously pursued under Elizabeth, formally legalised under James the First, confirmed and rendered irrevocable by the Cromwellian and Williamite wars. It was not a struggle with feudalism, but a general confiscation of the property of Irishmen (carried out without any attempt to avoid needless injustice), and the natural resistance which that confiscation provoked.

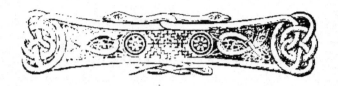

SECTION VI.

FREEMEN OWNING NO PROPERTY.

N further pursuance of our plan the next class to be considered is that composed of persons who were free but had little or no property, and consequently little or no power. Strictly speaking the collateral branches of most families, and persons thrust out of their *fines* by the operation of the law, and having no property, would fall within this description; but the persons I wish more particularly to gather within this convenient group, in order to separate them from those above them and from those below, were simply men who had become poor as the result of ordinary adverse circumstances, or of war, or of fines imposed for offences, or of want of industry. Their numbers fluctuated from various causes. They had rights by birth as members of their respective clans; but their want of property rendered and kept many of those rights in abeyance, unavailable, ineffectual. This was the only primary difference between them and their fellow clansmen who had property ; but in effect it was productive of many important differences ; so much so that in reality there was more in common between those people and the non-free than there was between them and propertied freemen, and many of them, abandoning all hope of recovering lost ground, deliberately threw up their clan status and their claims which poverty rendered practically worthless, and joined one or other of the non-free classes. Until they had done this, however, they were entitled to take part in the military muster of the clan, and had a number of other rights which any acquisition of property might enable them to realise, but which without property were empty. For example, they were entitled to feed stock on the Fearan Fine ; but so long as they had no stock the right was quite useless.

SECTION VII.

THE NON-FREE.

Sub-Section 1.—Preliminary.

INALLY, with regard to the last great division, the non-free. One is sorry to find that there were in Ireland in ancient times, as there have been in other countries in times ancient and modern, people who were not free, some of whom were not regarded as members of the clan (that is, not regarded as citizens), and had no birthright in any portion of the property of the clan. This was so in Christian as well as in pagan times. There were fluctuations both in the numbers who were not free and in the severity of their condition; and there is much reason for thinking that that condition hardly ever reached the degree of extreme abjectness.

The origin of servitude in Ireland is lost in the mist of pre-historic ages.   We are dependent on conjecture, the most probable being that the Milesians reduced to a condition of sufferance and servitude some portion of the Firbolg, Cruithni, and other races that had preceded them.   But the distinction between bond and free did not long correspond with racial distinction, because on the one hand many persons of the earlier races subsequently rose to rank and power and became scarcely distinguishable from the rest of the community; while on the other hand many persons of undoubted Milesian race sank, either in punishment of their personal crimes or as a result of war or other misfortune, to the very lowest rank of the non-free. Again, a distinction must be observed between individuals in bondage all over the country and Firbolg communities which occupied separate districts in some parts of the country until the Middle Ages.   These latter cannot be classed as non-free. They were long treated as an inferior race, defective in status and in political rights and power; their language and their manners in so far as they differed from those of the dominant race were considered, as usual in such cases, marks of inferiority; and they probably paid higher tributes than other people did. But they often proved themselves sturdy people, and in course of time the distinctions mentioned came to signify no more than the local characteristics at present observable in different parishes.

Without admitting that servitude in any form or

degree can be justified, or suggesting that any
number of wrongs can make a right, one is free
to observe that it is very hard to entirely eradicate
from any social system, and especially from one so
interwoven and complex as that of ancient Ireland,
a social condition which has taken deep root in it
and become part of it. Its continuance or discontinuance does not always rest with the free choice
of individuals: that choice may be overruled by
national requirements or what are deemed to be
such. There being no prisons or convict settlements
in Ireland, except where the natural prison afforded
by a small island was available, reduction to a
species of slavery, permanent or temporary, was
considered a reasonable punishment of criminals
guilty of capital offences but whose lives had been
spared, and of other criminals who could not or
would not satisfy the fines imposed upon them.
Slavery in such cases differed very little from trans-
portation or penal servitude. The taking of persons
as hostages, too, for various purposes in civil matters
was quite an ordinary proceeding in Ireland as in
other European countries in ancient times. When
any of these persons were forfeited the law entitled
the holder to keep them in servitude, permanently
or until they were redeemed or his claim satisfied
by their labour or otherwise according to its extent.
Cowards who deserted their clan in the day of trial
on the field of battle, or got wounded in the back
(while running away), lost their status however high
or low it might have been, and virtually lost with

it their freedom. And, unfortunately, war oftentimes in its consequences reduced the brave as well to slavery. It always at once increased the number of slaves and furnished a pretext for holding them. The wars with the Danes had this two-fold effect. Stress and trial came, however, and were neither prevented nor surmounted by the holding of slaves in increasing numbers. It is said that they were more numerous in the twelfth century than ever before, notwithstanding the condemnation of the Church. In England also in the same century slaves were very numerous, notwithstanding a similar condemnation. Slavery continued to exist in England to some extent down to the end of the sixteenth century, when it died a natural death; in Scotland down to the end of the eighteenth century, when it was abolished, in 1799, by the Act 39 George the Third, chapter 56; and in America, the land of the free, slavery existed until our own time.

In Ireland there were several grades in the non-free state, as in all classes of the free state; but there are three principal non-free classes distinguished in the laws, namely, the Bothachs, the Sen-Cleithes, and the Fuidhirs.

Sub-Section 2.—*Bothachs and Sen-Cleithes.*

HE word *Bothach* being connected with *bothan,* a cabin, it is inferred that the people called by this name were cottiers. *Sen-Cleithe* means *Old Stake,* or old adherent, and the people so called were the poor adherents and dependants of the flaiths, such as servants, herds, horse-boys, cart-boys, dog and hawk-boys, &c. Various writers describe both these classes as prisoners of war or their descendants. For my own part I believe that these two classes consisted wholly of persons born in the territory. Their very names indicate as much; so also does the class of business in which they were employed; and they were considered as in some sense members of the clan in whose territory they resided, which could hardly have been so had they been prisoners of war. But their connection with the clan did not go to the extent of giving them any birthright in the property of the clan; and I do not think they were entitled to arms or to take any part in the military muster. They had the right to

148

live in the territory as best they could by working
for any flaith or any other person who paid them
best.   They were not restricted as to whom they
should serve within the territory; but they were not
free to leave the territory except with permission, and
in practice they usually served the flaith.   They had
no political or clan rights, could neither sue nor
appear as witnesses, and were not free in the matter
of entering into contracts.   They could appear in a
court of justice only in the name of the flaith or other
person to whom they belonged, or whom they served,
or by obtaining from an aire of 'the tuath to which
they belonged permission to sue in his name.   In
this respect it was these people, not the céiles, who
resembled the *clientes* of ancient Rome.   They were
capable of acquiring land by contract, and when they
had done so they corresponded to the English *villeins*
of the Middle Ages.   With industry and economy
they might become wealthy, and with the acquisition
of wealth a certain progress was allowed upwards
towards liberty and an easier lot.   The distinction
of *saer* and *daer* was recognised in their condition ;
but it is not clear in what that distinction consisted,
unless the former represented legal status, which
wealth was the ordinary means of procuring.   Whenever any of them did by contract become land-holders
and wealthy they also acquired some social and
political rights, and could not be removed from their
lands without just cause and compensation for unexhausted improvements.   The main difference
between such men and the free clansmen was,

that while the clansmen's possession of land acquired by contract would in the course of ten years ripen into ownership, and cattle they had hired from the flaith and paid for would after seven years become their own, the non-free men had no such general law continually operating in their favour to this extent, but were kept to the terms of their contract because that was throughout their only title. A freeman sometimes paid a pretty heavy tribute for such land in the beginning; but in doing so he was gradually throwing off a burden from which he knew he would soon be entirely free. A non-free man paid a still heavier tribute, which was a rent in reality; and yet his burden continued undiminished, ever *wearisome*. And in every case of conflict the claim of the non-free man should give way to that of the clan or of a fully enfranchised member of the clan. The benefit of the principle of partnership was extended to these two classes also, enabling a number of them to put their small means together, take a piece of mountain side or other poor land and stock it on the system now called rundale, and by means of this property to acquire rights and the protection of the law. If five families had each become so wealthy as to own one hundred head of cattle, and had then formed a partnership or guild resembling the *fine* of the freemen, and appointed a chief or *flaith-fine*, they were entitled at once and thenceforth to be recognised as a portion of the clan; and then, but not till then, all the rules of kinship applied to them as to the free people. Until they had emancipated themselves by individual or joint wealth, or in some other way, they appear to have lived very much on the sufferance of the clan. The majority of them remained poor and had little occasion or inclination for testing the scope or existence of their rights. It is probable that the condition of even these was not on the whole worse than that of modern agricultural labourers. Their position was one of rightlessness rather than slavery; they were tolerated rather than bound.

Sub-Section 3.—The Fuidhirs.

UIDHIR was a name applied to all who did not belong to a clan, whether born in the territory or not. This was the lowest of the three classes of the non-free people. This class also was sub-divided into *saer* and *daer*, the *daer fuidhirs* being the class most closely resembling slaves. Even this lowest condition was not utterly hopeless; progress and promotion were possible, and indeed were in constant operation. But on the other hand the ranks of the fuidhirs continued to be recruited from various sources. It was here prisoners of war were to be found. The pagan Irish were wont to go on warlike expeditions to Britain and Gaul, and on their return to bring home, along with other booty, some of the

natives whom they reduced to slavery in Ireland. It
was in this way Saint Patrick was brought to Ireland,
and it was as a *daer fuidhir* he lived in Ireland in his
youth. Centuries after Saint Patrick's time the Irish
used to send to English ports and purchase children
as merchandise from their English parents, who sold
them freely. These children were brought up as
fuidhirs in Ireland. And, as already mentioned, the
ranks of the fuidhirs afforded a general refuge for con-
victs, fugitives from justice from other clans, tramps,
outcasts, and unfortunate persons of all sorts. A
freeman could remain in his own tuath and become
a daer fuidhir if all his property when given up was
insufficient to pay his debts—a species of bankruptcy
plus capitis diminutio. No fuidhir, saer or daer, was
entitled to bear arms, or to recover eric for the murder
of a member of his family, or to inherit property if
by any chance he found himself in a position in which
he would otherwise inherit. The law recognised the
fuidhirs in some respects, however, in certain matters
not fit to be stated here. The lowest of them were
regarded as intelligent persons, as human beings, not
mere chattels.

Fuidhirs and the non-free of all classes resided for
the most part on the flaith's land; for, apart from
the satisfaction of specific claims, the flaiths alone,
as a class, had the general right of keeping non-free
persons on their lands. This exclusive right originated
in the legal theory that they were public officers,
bound among other things to perform certain public
works requiring unskilled labour of a coarse kind,

and they were allowed to keep non-free people for the performance of these works for the benefit of the community, as with convict labour of the present day. In practice they mostly employed the fuidhirs in works for their personal benefit. They were free to give patches of land to the saer fuidhirs either on their official lands or on their private property. In practice they gave them patches on the common or waste land also, exacted rent for it as though it were private, and in this way appropriated that land. The land so given was usually the poorest, most inaccessible, and most difficult to utilise. The saer fuidhirs might, however, if they had the means, bargain with the flaith for good land and hold it for the term of one year, and during that term they could not be disturbed. For this land they paid him high rent, because he could charge them as much as he pleased, a thing he could not do with the clansmen. The daer fuidhirs, so long as they remained such, could hold no land whatever for any term, and no contract made with them had any binding effect. They worked for the flaith, and by means of their cheap labour he was able to cultivate his land, and some of the common land of the clan if it suited him. Both classes of fuidhirs helped the flaith to encroach on the property of the clan. Hence he had an interest in increasing the numbers of fuidhirs, and with their increase his dependence on the clan in some respects diminished. The moral and material interests of the free clansmen leant the other way. They disliked the presence and still more the increase of fuidhirs. The

policy of the law, too, was distinctly and uniformly
adverse to slavery and to the introduction and keeping
of fuidhirs, and it imposed some checks on the
practice. For the performance of servile labour
for the benefit of the community it allowed rather
than entitled chiefs and flaiths having control of
districts to keep a limited number of fuidhirs in
proportion to the size of their respective districts.
This particular restriction as to number does not
appear to have been operative. The law, however,
held the chief or flaith responsible to his clan and
to his king for all legal liabilities arising from the
acts of fuidhirs. It made his rank and privileges
depend on the number of céiles in his district. It
bound him to be ready when required to bring a
certain number of armed men into the field of
battle, and as the fuidhirs were neither bound nor
entitled to take part in military operations at all,
this demand could be satisfied only by free clansmen.
For all these reasons, however the flaith might
desire to increase the number of fuidhirs for his
personal advantage, he could do so directly at the
expense of the céiles only to a limited extent. In
other ways also the law discouraged the introduction
of fuidhirs ; and when they had been introduced it
favoured and facilitated the well-being and emanci-
pation of such of them as were not criminal. Therefore all families did not remain permanently in this
kind of servitude but gradually rose from a lower
to a higher degree according to a certain scale of
progress, unless they committed some crime which

would arrest that progress and cast them down again. This progress was arranged according to the time a fuidhir family had resided in the territory, and its thrift as evidenced by the amount of wealth acquired, subject to the effect of conduct. Though a flaith *might* not keep any bargain with a daer fuidhir, if as a fact he let land to him and *did* keep the bargain, a status began to be acquired. In the third generation the fuidhir family attained some partial connection with the clan and a foothold in the soil, so that they could not be driven away except for a crime. As time went on, if the progress was maintained, the rights of their descendants increased and expanded, they gradually intermarried with the clan and became indistinguishable from it, and their origin was forgotten.

In later times as the flaiths assumed the character of lords, all poor people, whether originally free or not, gravitated towards the condition of the ancient fuidhirs; and under Queen Elizabeth the majority of the Irish people were indiscriminately reduced to almost the same level. So they and their descendants remained for almost three centuries.

CHAPTER VI.

THE LAW OF DISTRAINING.

SECTION I.

INTRODUCTORY.

LET us now consider briefly the law of distress, that is the seizing of property for the satisfaction of debt. In its time it was substantially the most extensive and important part of the whole Brehon Code and in its operation affected the whole of it, being incidental to all litigation. That strange fact makes it interesting to us. It has besides some intrinsic points of interest. But the whole subject will not detain us at length proportioned to its ancient importance.

There had always been local customs regulating distress, but, as might be expected, neither were they all alike nor any one of them consistently observed even in the district to which it nominally belonged. The consequence was irregularity leading to injustice and sometimes to violence. The matter being so very important, a national convention was summoned and held, about a hundred years before the birth of Christ, on the hill of Uisneach, near the present town of Moate, in Westmeath, was attended by representative men from every province, and there a uniform system of distress drawn up and proposed by Sean (Shan), son of Aighe, a Connaughtman, was adopted for the whole country. This continued in force for nearly seventeen hundred years, and is the system now about to be briefly outlined.

SECTION II.

DEFINITION AND SCOPE.

ATHGABHAIL is the word translated *distress*. It means the resumption or recovery of either property or right of which one has been deprived. What was meant for a definition in the Gaelic is translated thus—" It is called Athgabhail, because through it advantage is obtained after disadvantage, property after the absence of property, possession after non-possession, truth after untruth, legality after illegality, justice after injustice, lawful possession after unlawful possession, right after wrong, order after disorder. Athgabhail is a general name for every security by which one recovers his right. Athgabhail is that which renders good to the good, which renders evil to the evil, which takes the guilty for his guilt."

Whatever the law commanded or prohibited, the command or prohibition, if not obeyed, was enforced by means of distress. It was a remedy of almost universal application. It was available for the recovery both of tributes and of ordinary debts, thus corresponding to both distress and the final execution of a writ of *fieri facias* in English law; but it was equally applicable, and as freely used, for the recovery of all sorts of mulcts, forfeitures, penalties, and fines, and for the satisfaction of every species of liability. And since the Brehons reduced all liabilities of whatsoever original nature to material value to be recovered by distress, the modern distinction between civil and criminal liability did not exist, and distress was applicable to every action and to every charge. Further, it was not alone the mode of executing a judgment, but also a mode of instituting an action. Hence the disproportionate importance of this subject and the enormous amount of space occupied by it in the Brehon Laws; and hence in the part of the Senchus Mōr dealing specially with it nearly all other branches of law are mentioned incidentally.

Whoever had any claim or complaint against another, either summoned that other or, by distraining, obliged that other to summon him before a brehon, who decided which party was in fault, and assessed the amount that person should pay to the other. There was no sheriff or other public officer to execute the distress and realise the amount assessed; the plaintiff, creditor, or person who had

gained the suit was obliged to do it himself; but in
doing so he was bound to take with him a law agent
in the character of a notary, together with witnesses,
as a guarantee that the requirements of the law
should be duly observed on both sides. He also
took with him such assistants as the occasion
suggested. A person distraining in this way does
not appear to have been any weaker or less successful than is the sheriff in our time. "If a man who
is sued evades justice, knowing the debt to be due
of him, double the debt is payable by him, and a fine
of five seds." This provision made the defendant
the party most interested in effecting a speedy
settlement.

SECTION III.

DISTRAINT BY FASTING.

ENERALLY a person before proceeding to distrain was bound to give certain notices. " A notice of five days is to be served on a debtor of the inferior grade, and then distress is to be taken from him." " A notice of ten days upon the debtor of chieftain grade." If the defendant was a chieftain, a flaith, a brehon, a bard, or a bishop, the plaintiff was obliged *to fast upon him* in addition. " Notice precedes every distress in the case of the inferior grades, except it be by persons of distinction or upon persons of distinction ; fasting precedes distress in their case." The *Troscead*, or fasting upon one, consisted in going to his house and waiting at his door a certain time without food. The text says, " He who refuses to cede what should be accorded to fasting, the judgment on him according to the Feini is that he pay double the thing for which he was fasted upon." This was a strong measure. And the commentary says, " If the plaintiff has fasted without receiving a pledge, he gets double the debt and double food." Again the text says, " He who fasts notwithstanding the offer of what should be accorded to him forfeits his legal right according to the decision of the Feini." Clearly the law did not suffer the mode of distress by fasting to be trifled with in any way. If the plaintiff, having duly fasted, did not within a certain time receive the satisfaction of his claim, or a pledge therefor, he forthwith distrained the goods as in the case of an ordinary defendant, *and distrained double the amount that would have satisfied him in the first instance.* Sir Henry Maine thought that fasting was regarded with a superstitious awe. I rather think the law, without superstition at all, was calculated to inspire a good deal of awe, and that the distinguished defendant, if he possibly could, paid the debt or gave a pledge in order to get the faster, as a dangerous nuisance, away from his door.

Distress by way of fasting, now so strange to us because so long obsolete, was clearly designed in the interests of honesty and of the poor as against the mighty. How or why it assumed this particular form is not known, and shall probably never be known. It was not peculiar to Ireland, however.

A system precisely similar has existed in India from time immemorial, and exists in some parts of that country at the present day. It is called "sitting *dhurna*." There are also other points of resemblance between the native laws of India and the Irish laws. India and Ireland are too far apart in space, time, and historical connection for these resemblances to be more than coincidences due to similarity of occasion, or to some common cause acting on the minds of men, or to chance.

SECTION IV.

GENERAL PROCEDURE.

RDINARY distress was of two kinds, " Distress with Time," and " Immediate Distress." In " distress with time," the thing seized was subject to an *anad*, that is, a respite, or stay, which was a period varying in duration according to fixed rules. " The stay of every distress with time is the delay in pound of every immediate distress which has no stay at all." The debtor or defendant, on giving a pledge or security to the plaintiff, received back the thing distrained, and retained it in his own possession during this period. Also if the defendant or debtor desired to test on any ground in a court of law the validity of the claim or the legality of the distress, he was allowed a certain time for this purpose, provided he gave security. The security was usually in the nature of a pledge, and might be any article of value which he could spare at the time without inconvenience, or it might be a member of his family. A person so given was treated as a hostage, not as a servant or slave. He was treated as his rank entitled him to be treated. If in the event he was forfeited, the plaintiff would acquire a vested interest in him to the extent of his claim, and might then take that much out of him by reducing him to slavery or in any other way he thought he could best effect his object. If the pledge offered was adequate as a security, the plaintiff was bound to accept it, whether it was likely to be useful to him or not ; for the law did not contemplate his making a profit out of it. If then the defendant did not bring the disputed point to a trial within the time allowed, as he had undertaken to do, the pledge became forfeited in satisfaction of the original claim.

The peculiarity of " immediate distress " was, that during the fixed period of the stay the thing distrained was not allowed to remain in the debtor's possession, but in that of the creditor, or in a *Forus* or pound of the district. This immediate distress was made, or might be made, if the plaintiff belonged to a higher rank than the defendant, and in some other circumstances ; and the distrainor might bring to his own pound goods to the value of his own honour-price.

In the case of " distress with time," if the debt was not paid at the end of the time, and in the case of " immediate distress," if the debt was not paid at once, the distrainor took away the things seized to his own residence or to pound according to circum-

stances, and served on the defendant a very explicit
notice. ".Three things are to be announced at the
residence of the defendant—the debt for which it
[the distress] was taken, the pound into which it was
put, and the law agent in whose presence it was
taken." In other words, the defendant was put in
possession of every material fact, in order that if so
disposed he might take the proper steps to secure
his interests. Treating of a negligent owner who at
such a time omitted to take any steps, the text says,
" To be asleep avails no one;" the commentary
says, " Sloth takes away his welfare ; " and an old
proverb says, " He is like a cow's tail, always
behind."

The distress remained in pound a certain time fixed
by law according to its nature ; and if it consisted
of cattle, as it usually did, the expenses of care and
keep accrued against it and was payable out of it for
this time ; but if any profit or advantage was derived
from the thing distrained, as the work of horses or
oxen or the milk of cows, this was set off against
the expenses. During the time in pound, which
was called a *dithim*, the owner of the property seized
might redeem it on paying the original debt, *plus* the
net cost incurred up to the time of redemption.
The plaintiff might, without risk, if he wished, allow
three days of grace in addition to the legal dithim.
At the end of the dithim, or days of grace if allowed,
the property, if not redeemed, *began* to be forfeited to
the plaintiff. It was not forfeited all at once even
then, but progressively at the rate of three seds per

day until the amount of the debt or fine or whatever
the principal sum was, with costs, was realised. If
the value of the thing distrained exactly equalled the
liabilities, the plaintiff took all and the matter was
at an end. If there was a surplus, it belonged to
the original owner; if a deficit, a further distress
might be made. The plaintiff would naturally be
disposed to seize too much rather than too little;
but the law discountenanced his harassing the defendant in this respect, and inflicted a heavy penalty
on any one who distrained unjustly, illegally, or with
needless oppression. A heavy penalty was also
incurred by any one who distrained where no debt
was due. These penalties were all fines, of course,
and the amount was doubled when the offence was
committed with guilty knowledge.

There were seven public pounds in the territory of
every clan. Of these the one most frequented was that
situated in the most secure place near the centre of
the territory, because in it the things detained were
safest from external thieves who could not be easily
brought to book. The laws contain elaborate rules
for the regulation of all classes of things in pound,
for liability in connection with accidents occurring to
cattle there, or having a disease going there, or taking
a disease in pound, and countless other possibilities;
and also special rules for every species of conduct
that might be indulged in by either of the parties,
and prescribing the proper course to pursue if the
distress had been carried out in any essential not in
accordance with the law. One specimen sentence

from the text will sufficiently indicate the scrupulous
care of the law. "Every necessity is blameless;
every improvement is lawful; every inadvertency
is venial; every wilful neglect is wrong."

There were times at which debtors were entitled
to certain exemptions from distress. On the death
of the Ard-Rīg of Erinn, and in Christian times on
the death of the successor of Saint Patrick, every
debtor in Ireland who needed and claimed it was
entitled to a year's exemption. On the death of the
king of a province there was exemption within that
province for three months. On the death of a rīg-
tuatha there was one month's exemption within that
tuath. But of course it did not follow that debtors
always took advantage of these periods of exemption.
They were meant only as temporary relief from hard
pressure, given to persons who claimed it *bonâ fide*.
Debtors applied to at a time of exemption, who
accepted notice, allowed themselves to be fasted
upon, or otherwise acknowledged or acquiesced in
the process going against them, and who were able
to pay, were not allowed at the last moment to avail
of the privilege of exemption, for that would be
unfair. Every person on whose death such a period
of grace would occur had during life the power of
giving protection against distress, and so temporarily
suspending the law, for the same length of time.

As regards the nature of the things distrained,
they were cattle for the most part, because they
could be driven and had not to be carried; but
cattle failing, any other farm produce was resorted

to, or any kind of property whatever. There was
an order, well and generally known, in which different
kinds of cattle should be taken in distress. Young
cattle that were not giving milk or otherwise essential
for the comfort of the family were liable, so far as
they existed, to be distrained before those that were
specially useful. In villages where smiths, carpenters,
shield-makers, and other mechanics lived, not by
land, but by their trades, the materials upon which
they worked or any other property found in their
possession might be distrained, but not their tools
or anything essential to the practice of their trades.
If a debtor or offender fled, leaving no property
behind him, the property of his *fine* might be seized
as though it were his own for the amount of the
debt or fine, and the members of the *fine* were left to
settle with the delinquent. People of the Bothach
and Sen-Cleithe classes having no property that could
be seized might be taken themselves in distress, and
were bound to pay the debt or fine by their labour.
While doing this their position towards the plaintiff
resembled that of the daer fuidhir towards the flaith.
When for crime or anything else fuidhirs became a
distrainor's object, he did not in the first instance
distrain them, because the flaith was responsible.
The law did not forbid him to chastise them, even
to death; but of course religious and moral considerations and public opinion restrained him ; and
on the whole it was the better and more usual
course to fetter them, and so deprive the flaith of
their services. The flaith might then either satisfy

the demand of the distrainor and enjoy his fuidhirs, or surrender the fuidhirs to the distrainor in the manner of the noxal surrender at Rome. · A fuidhir so surrendered had very likely to work harder for his new master than for his old; but probably he was better fed to enable him to do this. Though the rules relating to the distraint and surrender of human beings are numerous, and no doubt were sufficient in practice for those who applied them, they do not always convey the desired amount of information to us of a different age.

SECTION V.

CAPACITY.

N general, no one could levy a distress but a person on whom a distress could be levied. He should have a *lis* and a *macha* (= a fold and a farmyard) in the territory. Hence none of the non-free classes could distrain, except possibly such few of them as had acquired wealth and advanced a good way up the social scale. A stranger coming to levy a distress could not do so, under *Urradhus Law*, without bringing a native of the territory with him as surety, provided he could get one without fee. If he could get no native to become responsible for him without payment, and was unable or unwilling to pay, the law gave him other means of attaining his object, but not of so speedy a character. Those other means varied somewhat, the lodging of a substantial security being a common requirement. If a stranger failed to bring a surety in a case in which he was bound to bring one, or failed to lodge a security where he was allowed to do so, and attempted to distrain like a member of the clan, as by the cheap mode of fasting, not alone might he be evaded, but he was nonsuited and fined as an interloper. Under *Cāin Law*, however, a stranger could distrain directly without either a native surety or a security, provided he had a *lis* and a *macha* in his own native territory. And if in such a case in making his distress the stranger was evaded, the person evading him was fined; because the latter was in his own country where he had every facility for maintaining his rights, if he had rights. If instead of paying or giving a pledge, as the circumstances required, he attempted to baffle the stranger, the law stepped in for the protection of the stranger; and if in the result the stranger was able substantially to sustain his claim, it followed that the evasion of him was unjust and fraudulent, and it was punished as such.

Some modern exponents of the Brehon Laws tell us that only *flaith-fines* or heads of families could be sureties. Now this is another mistaken view. Not only were all the seventeen men of the *fine* eligible to become sureties, but they were *bound* in certain cases to become sureties for one another, and were liable as sureties even in cases where they had not expressly undertaken the responsibility. They were competent also to become sureties for other members of their own clan, but in this respect the *flaith-fine's* powers were more extensive than theirs ; and he could become a surety for a person outside the clan, which they could not. Kings, chiefs, brehons, officers of court, and others filling public positions were ineligible as sureties. The non-free were, of course, wholly ineligible.

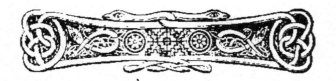

SECTION VI.

MINUTIÆ.

UCH is a general outline of the law of distress. There were many rules regarding the legality of certain distresses, the effect of exemption in different cases, and other differences, and curious and elaborate provisions for the execution of distress in the case of almost every animal and thing then held as property; and further numerous differences arose from the numerous classes of suitors and defendants, and the modifications of honour-price and consequently of liability caused by the progress of either or both parties in the scale of status, the arrest of that progress, and a great many other causes. The fines, distresses, stays, and all the processes of action were specifically adjusted to all these variations. There is hardly a way in which a wrong could be inflicted in country

life against which a special provision is not made,
hardly a thing relating to property or its use or abuse
for which a special rule is not given. These minute
rules are far too numerous and intricate for discussion
here. The same may be said of every branch of the
Brehon Laws. Even so friendly a critic as Dr.
Joyce has said it in his chapter on the subject,
where he contrasts unfavourably the minute spe-
cialism of the Brehon Laws with the adoption of
broad principles of general application. He does not
tell us, however, in what ancient laws the material
for this contrast can be found, in what ancient laws
broad principles have been actually adopted. It
is hard to find even in modern laws. He leaves
his readers to infer that the characteristic he con-
demns is more observable in the Irish than in other
ancient laws, and that the adoption of broad principles is easy and was easy to the brehons. Neither
of these assumptions would as a general rule be
correct. The tendency, however vain, to deal with
particular cases, to relieve where the shoe pinches,
is observable in all laws, past and present, even
in countries having legislatures at hand to enact,
amend, or abolish ; and as regards the liberty a
judge should take in interpreting law, most modern
judges uniformly and consistently shrink from laying
down broad principles or extending any rule beyond
the requirements of the case before them. Dr.
Joyce's criticism, therefore, while applicable to the
Brehon Laws, is also of far wider application than
Dr. Joyce's readers are led to suppose. It may be

observed, too, that for us this proneness to deal with particular cases and minute circumstances is not wholly a defect, since to it we owe our knowledge of many facts revealing to us the habits of the people.

CHAPTER VII.

CRIMINAL LAW.

SECTION I.

THE BOOK OF AICILL.

HE Senchus Mōr is the greatest work on Irish Law in general, civil and criminal. As it deals with the whole subject, the civil law occupies much more space than the criminal. Various branches of law are treated specially in separate treatises. The most important of these is the *Book of Aicill.* It is taken up mainly, but not exclusively, with what we now call criminal law, and may be regarded as the Irish criminal code; and it is this work that will mainly be referred to in explaining that code. It also contains some useful state-

ments of law relating to partnership, borrowing and
lending, and other transactions of civil life.

The whole of the Book of Aicill is composed of the
opinions or placita of two eminent men, illustrious
in law and in other respects: The first was King
Cormac mac Airt, otherwise called Cormac ua Cuinn;
the second was Cennfaeladh the Learned. Cormac
was one of the most deservedly celebrated of the
monarchs of ancient Erinn. He was Ard-Rīg from
A.D. 227 until 266 (according to others from 218 until
260). He was, as his names signify, the son of Art
and the grandson of Conn of the Hundred Battles,
both monarchs of Erinn, and he was the father of
Cairbrē who may be said to have succeeded him, the
very short reign of Eochaidh alone intervening. He
was also the father of Grainne, celebrated in the
Fenian poetry of Oisīn and his contemporaries.
In youth he was violent enough, perhaps un-
scrupulous in pursuit of power; but his subsequent life proved that his ambition rose from the
solid basis of ability to rule men; and to this
extent, as also by the use he made of power when
acquired, he justified himself. He was a great
reformer of the national institutions of his time,
civil and military, including the Feis of Tara; and
most of the traces of its former greatness now existing
at Tara are attributed to his time. Consistently
with his reforming spirit, he was a great patron of
literature, art, and industry, the first of whose
patronage we have undoubted evidence. He either
wrote himself or procured the writing of several

works on law, history, and other important subjects. Some of these works on subjects other than law were still extant so late as the seventeenth century, but appear to have been since destroyed or lost. Among the useful things for which the country was indebted to Cormac was the introduction of the water-mill. He had the first mill erected on a small stream on the slope of Tara. He was a man in many respects far in advance of his time. Though living long before Saint Patrick's arrival, and king of a pagan nation, there is reason for thinking that he was a believer in Christianity before his death. He at all events ceased to believe in the pagan gods.

> "Crom Cruach and his sub-gods twelve,"
>   Said Cormac, "are but craven treene :
> The axe that made them, haft and helve,
>   Had worthier of our worship been.
>
> "But He who made the tree to grow,
>   And hid in earth the iron stone,
> And made the man with mind to know
>   The axe's use, is God alone.
>
> "Spread not the beds of Brugh for me
>   When restless death-bed's use is done,
> But bury me at Rosnaree,
>   And face me to the rising sun.
>
> "For all the kings that lie in Brugh
>   Put trust in gods of wood and stone ;
> And 'twas at Ross that I first knew
>   One, Unseen, who is God alone."

According to one Gaelic authority Cormac was the author of the text of the Book of Aicill throughout, and Cennfaeladh afterwards modified and commented on the whole of it, besides adding some of the case law which had grown up in the interval. And I am inclined to think that this view is correct. However, the introduction to the Book of Aicill gives a different account, and naturally it is that usually accepted. It begins thus:—"The place of this book is Aicill, close to Tara, and its time is the time of Coirpri Lifechair (Carbre of the Liffey), the son of Cormac, and its author is Cormac, and the cause of its having been composed was the blinding of the eye of Cormac by Aengus Gabhuaidech." Owing to the loss of his eye, Cormac became incapable under the Irish law of retaining the sovereignty, "because it is a prohibited thing for one with a blemish to be king at Tara." The sovereignty was transferred to his son, after a temporary usurper had been got rid of, and Cormac retired to Aicill, now called Skreen, near Tara. It is stated that in difficult cases he was consulted by his son the young king. However this may be, a great deal of the Book of Aicill is written as if in answer to questions submitted, and the answer in each case begins with the words, "My son, that thou mayest know."

It was on account of this injury to his eye that Cormac expelled the Deisi from the district in Meath still from them called Deece, and drove them to Munster where they settled and gave their name to a district there also.

Having told where, when, on what occasion, and by whom, the book was first written, the introduction proceeds :—" These were the place and time of it as far as regards Cormac. But as regards Cennfaeladh, its place is Daire Lurain (now Derryloran, in Tyrone), and its time was the time of Domhnall, son of Aedh, son of Ainmirê; and its author was Cennfaeladh, son of Oilell, and the cause of its being composed was that part of his brain was taken out of his [Cennfaeladh's] head after it had been split in the battle of Magh Rath." The Domhnall (Donal) in whose reign this occurred was monarch of Ireland and fought the battle of Magh Rath (now Anglicised *Moira*) in A.D. 634 (? 642) against Congal Claen, king of Uladh.

The foregoing statements are remarkably clear and explicit. They represent the Book of Aicill as the production of two authors, one writing in the third century, the other in the seventh. Notwithstanding this, Sir Henry Maine, the standard authority on ancient law, in his learned discoveries of " village communities " where they never existed, represents Cennfaeladh as *assisting* Cormac! Worse still, I find an Irish author saying gravely that Cormac was just the man to appreciate Cennfaeladh's services! Granted that Cormac was highly endowed, still the power of appreciating services rendered more than three hundred years after his own death can hardly be conceded even to Cormac mac Airt; and if he had such power, any express recognition of Cennfaeladh's services would then have been rather premature.

We are told that Cennfaeladh (*Kenfaela*) was a

soldier, not a lawyer. I would rather describe him
as a soldier *and* a lawyer, and much besides. Having
been wounded in the battle of Moira, the commentary
goes on to say of him, "And Cennfaeladh was
brought to the house of Bricin of Tuam Drecain
(now Toomregan, in Cavan) at the meeting of the
three streets, between the houses of three ollamhs.
And there were three schools in the town, a school
of literature, a school of law, and a school of poetry.
And whatever he used to hear rehearsed in the three
schools every day, he had by heart every night ; and
he put a fine thread of poetry about them, and wrote
them on slates and tablets, and transcribed them
into a paper book." This was the way in which
Cennfaeladh spent his time while recovering from
his severe wound; and there is a characteristic
explanation given of his wonderful memory, namely,
that the brain of forgetfulness had been taken out of
his head by the sword by which he had been wounded.
Throughout the *Ancient Laws* occasional touches of
fancy like this are met with, thrown in apparently
by way of ornament, and possibly as an assistance
to young students in learning these laws. Saint
Bricin kept a school at Tuam Drecain ; and Cennfaeladh appears to have done part of his work there
and part at Derryloran.

Commentaries written by lawyers of later times
run through the Book of Aicill as through the Senchus Mōr. According to these, the part of the Book
of Aicill in which occur the introductory words,
"My son, that thou mayest know," and the part

called "the exemptions," are all the work of Cormac, and the remainder of the book is the work of Cennfaeladh.   Cennfaeladh re-wrote the whole work, and in doing so he probably modernised it to some extent in effect and in form of expression, and harmonised it with the requirements of Christianity after the example of the Senchus Mōr.   One may say in our present language that Cennfaeladh brought out a new and revised edition of King Cormac's work.

SECTION II.

THE LAW THEREIN LAID LOWN.

T is commonly said that no distinction existed in the Irish laws between civil and criminal liability. A distinction did exist, but it was not the same as that in English jurisprudence. The common punishment of all sorts of crimes and all sorts of civil wrongs was indeed a fine, varying in amount according to the nature of the act, to be levied on the property of the offender like a civil debt. All proceedings, whether for a crime, a tort, or a breach of contract, were identical in origin and prosecuted by the same persons and generally in the same manner. The State did not prosecute, but left individuals to prosecute in criminal as well as to sue in civil cases. The law did not set up crime as a species of liability distinct from civil wrong. Still there were important

points in which criminal differed from civil liability.
It differed first in the moral nature of the act by
which it was incurred ; and this was a legal difference so far as the law enforced it. There is here a
confusing of law with morality, which some English
legal authorities are at such pains to keep asunder
or in antagonism. Theirs is trouble ill-bestowed,
and vainly, because its object is unnatural. Until
human nature itself is changed law and morality
will, in spite of lawyers' theories, be in fact and be
generally considered closely related. And it can
hardly be denied that wilful civil wrong is oftentimes
the medium of base moral crime. Another difference,
sometimes of importance, was, that, in civil cases
the defendant frequently had the right of choosing
the judge. This arose from any one of certain
causes. For example, if the plaintiff distrained as
the first step in an action, as he might do when his
claim was for a liquidated amount, the defendant
was driven to the necessity of either submitting to
the distress or taking the case before a brehon.
Criminal cases, the amount obtainable not being
liquidated, had to be submitted to a brehon in the
first instance, and hence the person against whom
a crime had as a fact been committed chose the
brehon. Then the subsequent effects upon status
and legal competence were entirely different.

Persons against whom crimes had been committed,
or if they had been killed their immediate relatives,
were left to sue out redress, just as in civil cases,
by summoning the offender to appear before a

brehon, who heard the case and assessed, according
to the principles of law and justice, the amount of
fine that should be paid as compensation; and then,
if the defendant did not pay immediately, by levying
a distress on his goods. There were no prisons,
except in communities to which small islands or
other natural prisons belonged, and there were
hardly any public servants who could correctly be
called police or detectives. The people were their
own police, and their activity in that character was
spurred and sharpened by the knowledge that a sept
had to pay for a secret crime committed in the part
of the territory assigned to it, unless it were shown
that the crime had been committed by an outsider.
This liability of the sept continued so long as the
criminal lived, whether his crime was one against
person or gainst property. But on his death
happening, whether as punishment for the crime or
from natural causes, a difference arose. If the crime
was purely personal, the liability of the sept was at
an end, for " the crime dies with the criminal; " but
if it had caused damage or loss of property, the sept
still remained liable for this net loss. Every clan
and every clansman had a direct monetary interest
in the suppression and prevention of crime. The
higher motives by which Irishmen were undoubtedly
actuated were, however, far more effectual. The
whole public feeling of the community was entirely
in support of the law—a signal proof of its suitability.
Evasion of law and concealment of lawbreakers,
which alien laws afterwards made so popular in

Ireland, were then little known. Both in popular estimation and in fact the honour and the interests of all, of community and individual, were involved in the maintenance of the law. Law supported by public opinion, powerful because so inspired, powerful because unanimous, was difficult to evade or resist, though there were no men in livery to enforce it. It so strongly armed an injured person, and so utterly paralysed an offender, that an escape from justice was hardly possible. The only way in which it was possible was by running away, leaving all one's property behind him, and sinking into slavery in a strange place; and this in effect was a severe punishment rather than an escape. So long as an offender had property, the motive for flight was not so strong as it is with a criminal of the present day; for the brehons do not appear to have taken on themselves to pronounce the death sentence at all, but only the amount of compensation. In some cases of a criminal caught in the act, the person against whom he was offending had a right to fetter him and detain him wherever he pleased until judgment was pronounced and satisfied.

If a criminal did abscond without paying the penalty of his crimes, any property he left behind him was applied to the payment of it *pro tanto*. If not fully satisfied, the liability for the remainder fell first upon the criminal's immediate relatives who were entitled to inherit his property. If not satisfied by them, it extended throughout the *fine* and the sept even to the clan if necessary. The only way in which the immediate relatives, being able to pay, could escape liability was by giving up the offender to the injured family. The right to recover and the liabilty to pay were alike based on the rules of kinship explained in connection with the clan system.

The names of the fines are retained untranslated, for reasons already mentioned. They were *eiric* or *eric*, reparation ; *einachlan*, honour-price (not strictly a fine) ; *dire*, fine ; *coirpdire*, body-fine ; *smacht*, usually a fine of five seds ; and *airer*, a fine amounting to one-seventh of the honour-price. Eric is defined as the fine for separating body from soul, that is for killing, whether murder or manslaughter. But of course the amount of it was not the same in these cases; for one of the most important distinctions made by the law in crimes was the presence or absence of intention. A man who happened by pure accident to kill another who was about his lawful business did not go wholly unpunished, as such a one does here at the present time. Having destroyed human life and inflicted an irreparable injury on a family, he had to pay eric to the family of the deceased, and so alleviate suffering by sharing it. But one who committed wilful murder with malice aforethought had to pay at least a double fine. As an English lawyer would express it, the eric for murder was double that for manslaughter. So the translators tell us, and they are supported by the commentary which says, " The double of honour-price is due to each and every person for the crime of secret murder." Still it is conceivable that the word *diabalta* might be as correctly translated *two-fold*; for there were really two fines imposed, in some cases three, and they were not always equal in amount as the word *double* implies, since they started from different bases and the amount of each was affected by a different status and a somewhat different combination of circumstances. I find it laid down in one place that there were three fines imposed on a murderer, (1) his own honour-price; (2) seven cumhals for the homicide itself; (3) twice seven cumhals if malice was proved. I do not know of what rank this is said; but the actual amounts were affected by the different ranks, as well as by the facts and peculiar circumstances of each particular case, and each of the parts of the fine was in every case the subject of a separate and independent calculation.

Some loosely written passages in the commentaries have been interpreted, I think incorrectly, as meaning that the amount of fine which a murderer had to pay in order to avoid the liability of being put to death was his own honour-price. This would mean that the eric of the slain would always be equal to the honour-price of the murderer; a thing which, so far from being the rule, could hardly ever occur in practice. It could occur only when the slayer and his victim belonged to precisely the same rank *and* there were no circumstances to either extenuate or aggravate the guilt. As these essential conditions could scarcely ever be satisfied, the amount of simple eric could scarcely ever tally with the murderer's honour-price. But still less could the double and triple eric mentioned so tally. Eric and honour-price were, both in theory and in fact, wholly different things. Eric was strictly a fine regarded from the point of view of the party who had to pay it; but its amount was determined not by his status but by that of the victim. Honour-price was the assessed value of status; and, as applied to fines, the status in this case might be that of the criminal.

The eric (=reparation) was given, as its name imports, to the relatives of the person slain, in the proportion in which they were entitled to inherit his property, that being also in accordance with the degree of relationship, and usually with the degree in which those persons were really sufferers. In the Middle Ages all the parts of the fine were called comprehensively eric, and were so distributed. While Ireland had a monarch of her own he was entitled to one-third of the honour-price of every murderer in Ireland. If he was a " king with opposition," that is one whose title was disputed, he was entitled to only half this amount.

The same law that arranged the different ranks of society, and fixed their respective rights, privileges, and liabilities, affixed also to each rank, from king to plebeian, a measure of value called honour-price. By crime, and by breach of contract, this honour-price was forfeited, wholly or partially according to the magnitude of the wrong, to the person injured, with or without fines of other denomination accord-

ing to circumstances. By the taking of human life
in any way, and by a few other capital crimes, the
whole of the honour-price was forfeited, and if not
paid and accepted in satisfaction the injured person
or family had a right to put the criminal to death.
Even should the criminal be allowed to live, if no
satisfaction was rendered his tribal status was completely gone. In the case of certain peculiarly vile
crimes, which need not be further specified here,
the criminal was expelled from the clan and from
the territory, even though the fine had been recovered. A habitual criminal might also be expelled, and by expelling him, and lodging a security
against his future misdeeds, his relatives could free
themselves from responsibility. A person so expelled became an outlaw, with no status or right
whatever, no legal capacity, and no protection from
the law, and any one who gave him food or shelter
became liable for his crimes. There was little
danger of any one succouring him, for in general
public feeling was as much against him as the law,
and he was forced to go into a strange place, where
he could only sink into the lowest rank of fuidhirs.
If he still haunted the territory of the clan, and
continued his crimes there, he was proclaimed in
the public assembly of the clan. After this any
one might kill him as a wild beast or a mad dog.
Crimes less than capital, as lying, perjury, fraud,
and in the case of a judge a false judgment, if committed three times deprived the offender of half his
honour-price, if committed any more deprived him

of the whole of it. Accomplices in crime, and those who aided and abetted crime, were dealt with almost as severely as the actual criminal. In no case was the fine imposed on a criminal the full measure of the punishment. Besides the general odium, there resulted a loss of status with its legal consequences of disqualification for holding public office, for suing, for being a witness, a surety, a juror, and incapacity to inherit land. How long this condition lasted is not stated; but it was not permanent.

The amount of a fine, under whatever name it came, was not determined by abstract principles of general application, but in each case by the facts proper to that case. The maintenance of the law and of private rights were indeed principles affecting the ultimate decision; but the chief factors in determining the amount of penalty for any given crime were, (1) the damage done; (2) the status of the injured person; (3) the status of the criminal; (4) the accompanying circumstances. The result was that like punishments did not always follow like crimes. The rules of law on the subject were necessarily very numerous and complicated, owing to the great number of classes into which society was divided and the consequent variations in status and honour-price; and although when the facts were clearly ascertained the proper amount of a fine may be said to have been a matter of calculation, yet it was a calculation which required considerable technical skill, as did also the ascertainment of the facts. A fine for a breach of contract was generally more simple, as it would depend largely on the terms of the contract broken.

In adjusting punishment to rank, account was taken also of professional character. The clergy, for instance, were far more severely punished than the laity—a fact showing, if it were necessary, that Saint Patrick did not abuse his influence when the laws were being drawn up. When a lay criminal had paid the eric or other fine imposed upon him, he rested under a stigma and loss of status for some time; but after this probationary period he recovered his honour-price. A convicted clergyman could never recover his honour-price, could never regain his former status; and from the state of his surroundings he was scarcely free to do anything else but retire from the world and do penance.

Rank did not always affect the amount of fine in the same way. A man of high rank was always fined more than a man of low rank in a like case. An offence against property committed upon a poor clansman who could ill afford it, was punished more severely than a similar offence upon a wealthy person. An assault or other personal outrage upon a person of rank was more severely punished than a similar offence upon an ordinary person.

Fines, like other payments, were all paid in kind. When the offence was one against property, and the fine was small, it was usually *arra*, that is *generic*, a quantity of property of the same kind as that stolen or damaged. For damage done to bees,

14

for example, the fine would be so many *kishes* (hives). In the case of property not so conveniently divided as bees, the quantities were usually measured in *seds* or in *screpalls*. A screpall was $\frac{1}{21}$th of the value of a cow. A large fine was *anarra*, *not* generic, not consisting of the same substances as those stolen or injured. It was usually adjudged to be paid in three different substances, as one-third in horned cattle, one-third in horses, one-third in silver. If in corn it would be one-third in wheat, one-third in oats, and one-third in barley. In fixing the *kinds* the brehon should have regard to the actual nature of the defendant's property. A judgment obtained by a plaintiff for the payment to him of a fine in a particular kind of property which the defendant did not possess was called a "blind nut," because it was ineffectual; and if it had been obtained un-fairly or for any sinister purpose it debarred the plaintiff from seeking a different judgment. When the liability was of a civil nature, but arose in the absence of any express agreement between the parties, the judgment was a general one, and the defendant was allowed to pay the fine in whatever material he could most conveniently spare. The plaintiff had to be satisfied, because the law con-sidered that if he had desired to secure for himself on a foreseen event a fine of a particular description, he ought to have made a bargain to that effect.

For an offence committed against himself, as distinguished from one against his property, the plaintiff obtained a general judgment which he was entitled to realise out of any property belonging to the defendant that he pleased. If the defendant preferred to pay in any particular kind, he should offer it promptly. The judgments ran—so many screpalls for a white wound, so many for a red wound, so many for a lump blow, so many for a wound which left a mark on the face, so many for one which left no mark. These amounts, however, were only fixed by the law for the brehon's guidance, and subject to increase or diminution by him according as negligence on the one side, contributary negligence on the other, provocation, self-defence, accident, or any other modifying element appeared in the case. Subject to such modifications, minute regulations are laid down for a vast number of conditions, occupations, and circumstances, and the various offences connected with them. Of crimes directly against the person, the more serious have been noticed in connection with eric and honour-price. All fines were what we should consider heavy, fines for crimes against the person especially so. A fine of two cows was very heavy for a lump blow, that is, a blow which raised a lump but did not draw blood. And the same was the fine inflicted for shaving a man against his will. I think it meant shaving his head. This was an ignominious form of punishment in England under Alfred, and it may have been so in Ireland as well, and therefore if done without authority of law it would be particularly outrageous. It must also have been peculiarly aggravating among a people like the Irish who took pride in their long hair. They knew how to punish it at all events. But it must be remembered that the amount of a fine was affected by the status of the criminal as well as by that of the person he had outraged, and the heavy fines stated in the text applied only to *aires* or persons of full status who, as such, were wealthy. It is also fair to point out that the punishments of ancient laws were generally severe, some of them much more so than those of the Irish laws. Take a specimen from the dooms of Alfred, the model English king:—"He who curseth his father or mother, let him perish by death."

If one wounded a man who was the sole support of a family, he was fined for the actual injury, he had to pay for the medical and surgical attendance, and he had to pay a substitute to carry on the injured person's business. Fines are laid down for injury resulting in the loss of limbs, eyes, and all members; and the amount was affected by, among other things, the use the person was accustomed to make of the limb before its injury. One who knocked the nail off the finger of a harper was fined more than if he had inflicted a similar injury upon any other person. Another element sometimes presenting itself in calculating the amount of fine to be paid for a crime was, that the accused might have been provoked by some antecedent crime of the accuser. If this was shown, and the previous offence was one of which the law took cognizance, the judge was allowed to apply the principle of set-off, as were the judges of England according to the *Laws of Henry the First.*

Fines are carefully laid down for cattle-stealing, the laceration or injury of living cattle by dogs or otherwise, and trespass upon land. This latter was divided into man-trespass and beast-trespass. The forms of man-trespass most frequently dealt with were felling trees on another person's land and taking them away, and cutting turf, rushes, &c., on another person's land. The form of beast-trespass most severely dealt with was that of pigs, because they not alone eat and trample upon a crop but root it out of the earth. For the trespass of a large pig in a growing crop the fine was a sack of corn. For the trespass of a middle-sized pig, half a sack. For the trespass of a sucking-pig, two *māms*, a *mām* being all the corn it is possible to raise between the two hands. Other matters of frequent occurrence in the laws are the bites and other forms of damage done by dogs; meddling with another person's bees; bees stinging strangers and blinding or killing them ; bees stinging the various kinds of cattle and driving them furious; dangers connected with the felling of timber, the building of houses, the works of smiths, weavers, threshers, millers, kiln owners, &c. If an idler coming uninvited about such works was accidentally struck, he should put up with his injury. A person on lawful business so struck should be fully compensated ; unless he had been warned, either expressly or by the noise of the work, and had disregarded the warning. Rules are also laid down for cases of fellow-workmen hurting one another. There are rules regarding the management of horses at a fair, and liability arising from damage done by them ; also regarding damage done by vicious horses. Many rules relate to ferries, there having been more water in the country formerly than now, and fewer bridges. There are rules regarding the mistakes and mal-practices of doctors. It appears that, unless under special agreement, a doctor could recover his fee only on the patient getting well. In a dangerous case in which an operation, as the amputation of a limb, became necessary, a doctor should take an indemnity against liability for the fatal termination of his operation. If he was not a duly qualified doctor he should give notice of that fact to the patient and his family. If one suffered, from crime or accident, an injury at first apparently slight, and got judgment for a small amount, and afterwards, without fault of the doctor, the injury " came against " the patient seriously, or became fatal, the person to blame was liable to a second trial, but in this regard would be had to the amount recovered under the previous judgment.

In short, here as elsewhere, the brehons endeavour to deal with all cases and all varieties of circumstances. They lay down special rules for every relation of life known in their time and every detail of social and domestic economy, and some rules relating to conditions so obsolete that their nature can now only be conjectured.

SECTION III.

CAPITAL PUNISHMENT.

THE fact that the Irish took compensation for murder instead of putting the murderer to death, has been stupidly laid hold of by some English authors and journalists as a national reproach, which, with characteristic courtesy, instead of overlooking as a thing of the dead past, they delight to utilise. It would be foreign to my present undertaking to discuss the abstract question, whether it is better on the one hand when one man has been killed to kill another and make no reparation to the sufferers by the first death, or on the other hand, to make reparation out of the murderer's property and spare his life. The latter course is *prima facie* the more humane, and either side of the question is quite arguable. It is with the superior critics I am for the moment concerned. Those gentlemen with

their readiness to criticise must be assumed to
know, and with that delicacy of conscience by
which they profess to be moved might be expected
to state, that the law of making reparation for
murder, be it good or bad, so far from being
peculiarly Irish, was formerly almost universal. It
was practised by, amongst others, their own ancestors—that is, if it be possible to determine who
were the ancestors of a hybrid people. It was
practised by the ancient Greeks, and in later times
by the Lombards, Gauls, Franks, Swedes, Danes,
Germans, and Saxons, the only difference being that
while the laws of those nations imposed fixed and
rigid fines for the murder of specified persons, the
Irish laws always allowed fines to be reduced or
increased by mitigating or aggravating circumstances. The Anglo-Saxons called the price or
value set upon a man his *wergild*, the same as the
German *wehrgeld*, the amount of which depended
mainly upon rank and the amount of property
possessed, and the nature of which does not seem
to have at all differed from the Irish honour-price.
The *wergild* is met with all through the old English
laws. But one had better be specific. It is met
with in the laws of Ine, of Alfred, of Edward the
Elder, of Æthelstan, and of Edmund, who appears
to have encroached upon it. He did not extinguish
it, however, for it appears in the laws of Ethelred,
of Cnut, of Edward the Confessor, and of William
the Conqueror; in the latter case the mode of its
distribution being laid down, the largest portion

being given to the widow of the man slain, and the remainder divided among his nearest surviving relatives. In the code or compilation called the *Laws of Henry the First*, the *wergild* appears as a clearly recognised part of the existing law, and the amount of it is specified for parricide and all the graver crimes committed by or against the various classes from king to peasant ; and the only variation of the fixed amounts that appears to have been allowed was, that they might be increased if the crimes had been committed on holy days, as Sunday, Ascension Day, Lady Day, All Saints' Day, &c.

These are historical facts recorded on authority which Englishmen would be the last in the world to question. Any one may read them, and it is an Englishman's duty to know and remember them when he feels tempted to make himself ridiculous by thanking God that he is not like the rest of men, and assuming sanctimonious airs, to which nobody but himself thinks he is entitled. It may be said that they are very ancient facts. So are the Brehon Laws. It was possible to compound a felony in England until the power to do so was abolished in 1819 by the now meaningless looking statute, 59 George the Third, chapter 46. That is not very ancient. Until 7 and 8 George the Fourth, chapter 28, was passed, a man who' fled from trial, forfeited all his goods and chattels, *even though as the result of the trial he was acquitted.* That is not very ancient. Until 54 George the Third, chapter 146, the dead bodies of victims of the law were not sacred. Of

course it will be argued, and with truth, that many
things are possible under the law long after they
have ceased to be practised ; and, you know, every
conceivable excuse must be urged when the English
character is assailed. Excuses exist only for English
consumption. It never at any time was possible
to say of the courts of the brehons as Hallam says
of the courts of the Tudors, that they were " little
better than caverns of murderers." And if we turn
to what was actually practised in England in times
still more modern, what do we find ? We find that
a prisoner was not allowed before his trial to know
anything of the case against him, was not even told
the name of his accuser, was given no reasonable
opportunity for preparing his defence, while the
State paid for preparing the case against him ; and
if found guilty—as well he might be in such circumstances, though innocent—the sentence might
be death, or breaking of limbs, or stretching on the
wheel, or cutting out of his tongue, or gouging out
of his eyes, or clipping of his ears, or a combination
of several of these. I should be sorry to suggest
that there is a decent Englishman living to-day who
would not shudder and blush at the long catalogue
of unfortunate human beings who, under every one
of the four Georges, were after every assizes put to
death or subjected to the other grim barbarities
mentioned, in many cases for offences for which a
flogging or a month's imprisonment is now deemed
sufficient punishment. Those punishments were so
many fragments of the savage law of vengeance,

carried out, not by the sufferer or his friends, nor in their interest, but by the State, and as likely as not carried out on the wrong persons. They are recalled in no spirit of antipathy to the Saxon, for though a Gael of the purest blood I entertain none; nor are they recalled to make him ashamed of his ancestors, for we all have enough to do to keep our own lives pure; but they are recalled as common knowledge which it is his special duty to possess, and the possession of which should moderate his conceit to becoming limits, since it shows that, after all, he is not so much superior to the rest of men, and that in this very matter in which he presumes so much, we have at least as good ground for pride. No doubt it is very good of him to desire that his ancestors should be spoken of only with charity. We quite agree—because they need it. For ours all we desire is justice. His reproach amounts in substance to this, that our ancestors were more humane than his, and have not so much innocent blood on their heads. But for his modesty no doubt he would add, in further proof of our national depravity, that our ancestors never had any witches to burn, and never made the schoolmaster, as such, a criminal. It would be to his advantage to remember, what he cannot prevent the world at large from knowing, that his present perfection in this particular, as in many others of which he boasts, has not been evolved from his own inner essence, but is due to external influences acting on him, sometimes acting very much against his will. There is ample

space in this world even for Saxon mediocrity in
borrowed Norman plumes; but it must not disregard
the fitness of things and presume to lecture where it
can more profitably learn.

Still, having resented cant, one is free to say that
possibly the principle of reparation would have given
place to the death penalty as in England, or (more
likely) would have been made an accompaniment of
the death penalty as in France, had Ireland been
ruled as those countries were by a competent central
government. For centuries its nominal government
was incompetent and external.

At a very early period in Ireland, as elsewhere,
the acceptance of eric may have been optional.
The family whose member had been murdered
might not seek eric, or might reject it if offered,
and proceed to revenge. Also, if a murderer unable
to pay eric was surrendered by his relatives to the
family of his victim, the latter might kill him if they
pleased if nobody intervened to save his life by
paying the eric. I believe the Brehon Laws do not
expressly forbid persons suffering actual personal
outrage to chastise a criminal caught redhanded ;
and there is even a passage translated in these
words : "A person who came to inflict a wound
on the body may be safely killed when unknown
and without a name, and when there was no power
to arrest him at the time of committing the trespass."
The English law in force this day contains a precisely similar tacit allowance, even to the extent of
taking life. Then it must be remembered that we

possess not the whole Brehon Laws as the people understood them, but only the parts written for the guidance of judges and lawyers in the trial and treatment of offences brought before them, that much of human life never came before them, and that some abstract considerations which occur to us many centuries after date either did not occur to them at all or did not clamour for settlement.

It is quite possible for the law of reparation and *lex talionis*, or law of personal vengeance, to exist side by side in the same country as alternative modes of redress. Indeed, they appear to have so existed in many countries. Eric itself may be regarded as a species of retaliation as we use that word ; but it was a distinct improvement on the strict *talio* of the Roman Law—*Si quis membrum fregit, ni cum eo placit, talio esto.* In pagan Ireland, as far as I have been able to gather, a wilful murderer was regarded as lost soul and body, and possibly even though eric had been obtained his life might or might not be taken at the will of the prosecutor. It is pointed out with special care in the commentaries of the Senchus Mōr that the change effected by Saint Patrick was, to let the murderer be put to death as before if no eric could be obtained, but *to send his soul to heaven ;* and it adds, " for retaliation prevailed in Ireland before Patrick, and Patrick brought forgiveness with him." " At this day we keep between forgiveness and retaliation, for as at present no one has the power of obtaining heaven, as Patrick had at that day, so no one is put to death for his intentional

crimes as long as eric-fine is obtained ; and wherever
eric-fine is not obtained he is put to death for his
intentional crimes, and placed on the sea for his
ignorant crimes and unlawful obstructions." It
might be inferred from some strong expressions in
Dubhthach's poems that eric had been abolished
and the death penalty substituted, as where he says,
" Let every one die who kills a human being ; " and
again, " Every living person who inflicts death shall
suffer death." Since, however, the immediately
succeeding generations of lawyers did not at all
understand that eric had been abolished, it in fact
was not abolished, and it would be idle for us to
understand its abolition.

There is great diversity of opinion among modern
writers who have noticed the Brehon Laws as to the
frequency or infrequency of capital punishment in
ancient Ireland. One says the death penalty was
the standing rule, and the payment of eric the exception ; while another says that eric was nearly always
paid in order to spare human life, and that therefore
the death penalty was rarely inflicted, except for high
crimes against the king or the state institutions, or
the disturbance of a public assembly. I rather
incline to agree with the latter view ; first, because
of several passages in the law to the effect that no
one is to be put to death as long as eric is obtained,
that an assailant is not to be killed if he is known or
can be arrested, and so on ; and secondly, because I
have not found in the law any rules subject to which
the death penalty should be carried out. Hanging

is mentioned as having been carried out in political but not in private cases. If capital punishment was at all frequent, those laws, with their proneness to detail, would certainly contain some such rules. One of the punishments mentioned incidentally was that of placing a man on the open sea, on some small punt or wicker basket presumably. This was rather exposing a man to death than putting him to death. I cannot but think that some of the kindly Gael would be on the look-out for an unfortunate man so exposed, and, deeming his punishment sufficient, as soon as the coast was clear would come to his relief. There is ample evidence of various kinds that the whole public feeling of Ireland was opposed to capital punishment ; and still more was it opposed to the taking the law into one's own hands without the decision of a court. Such a popular sentiment was not law, of course, and never found a place in the law; but during and to the extent of its prevalence it was as good as law for all who obeyed it ; and, whatever their motive, in a country where the execution of the law rested with the people themselves, if they did not execute it the law was so far superseded. There was no public executioner ; and among a people who so respected the judgment of a brehon the want of a direct death sentence must have enfeebled the ordinary man going to imbrue his hands in his neighbour's blood, even though that neighbour was a murderer. For these reasons I conclude that, except for treason to the king and the state institutions, our forefathers rarely put criminals to death.

SECTION IV.

THE MAIGHIN DIGONA.

AIGHIN DIGONA was the name of a precinct of sanctuary secured by the law around the dwelling-house of every clansman, within which the owner and his family and property were inviolable. It was sometimes a cleared space the boundary of which was marked by trees or bushes ; but whether thus perceptible to the eye or not did not affect its reality. The English saying that every Englishman's house is his castle, is an illustration of the spirit that prompted the maighin digona. The sanctuary varied in extent with the owner's rank. In the case of a *bo-aire* it extended as far as he, while sitting at his house, could cast a *cnairsech*. This is differently described as a spear and as a sledgehammer. It was probably neither, but bore some resemblance to both. It consisted of a head of iron fastened on a wooden handle "twelve fists" in length. The hand was commonly used as a standard of measure, being considered four inches across the palm at the roots of the fingers, six inches across at the thumb with the thumb extended. On the end of the wooden handle was a *bocīn* (bokkeen) or horn fixed crosswise, just as the Irish peasants are to this day accustomed to fix bokkeens on the handles of the tools they use. One throw of this instrument determined the extent of the *bo-aire's* sanctuary, twice this for the *aire-desa*, and so on, the distance being doubled for each successive grade in the ascending scale. Four throws and three score (*i.e.* sixty-four throws) was the extent of the Rīg-Tuatha's sanctuary. This is said to have equalled a thousand paces. In some districts the sanctuaries of chiefs were measured by the sound of a bell or the crow of a cock. A provincial king might, if he pleased, assert sanctuary over the whole extent of the plain on which his dun stood. The bards and brehons appear to have had the same extent of sanctuary as the rīg-tuatha. In Christian times bishops appear to have had the same extent of sanctuary; whence, perhaps, it may be inferred that in pagan times the arch-druids were similarly favoured. An ollamh's wand carried round and over a fugitive anywhere protected him as did the maighin digona.

The owner of a maighin digona was empowered to extend its protection to a stranger flying from the

15

hue-and-cry; but no stranger could effectually avail of it without the owner's consent. If this consent was obtained, the effect of the extension was to save the stranger from the violent hands of his pursuers. They could not pursue or meddle with him further, but were obliged to resort to the legal methods of bringing him to justice. They could summon him before a brehon, and against this the sanctuary did not protect him at all. If they violated the protection by continuing the pursuit and abusing the fugitive, they incurred liability to the owner of the maighin digona.

The owner of a sanctuary was bound not to allow a fugitive to escape. " He who lets a criminal escape is himself a culprit." He might avert violence, but not defeat justice. When asserting his sanctuary he was bound to give the pursuer a guarantee that he would not allow the fugitive to escape; and if no actual guarantee was given the law presumed a guarantee, and held the owner of the sanctuary responsible for the original offence if he allowed the prisoner to escape.

CHAPTER VIII.

LEGES MINORES.

SECTION I.

MARRIAGE.

OGICALLY the subject of Marriage should have been discussed in connection with the account of the clan system. But not being essential to that account, its introduction there would have further confused a subject already sufficiently obscure.

Under the clan system one would expect to find the marriage laws very important and clearly laid down; yet, notwithstanding the domestic familiarity of the laws, the information given on the marriage relation is surprisingly scanty, and of a disappointing character

too. The ancient Celtic family was not constructed
like the modern Christian family, and it retained its
form for some time after the people had become
Christian. What precisely that form was, and what
the principle of construction, being matters involved
in our lack of knowledge of the clan system, are now
subjects of more or less wild conjecture. My own
impression is that in reference to the small private
circle which we should call the family, it is not so
much knowledge of the thing itself we lack as knowledge of the manner in which the clan organisation
produced such a condition of things that the law was
rarely invoked in matters which are of frequent
occurrence in modern litigation.

So far as the laws show, the marriage relation was
extremely loose, and divorce was as easy, and could
be obtained on as slight grounds, as is now the case
in some of the States of the American Union. It
appears to have been obtained more easily by the
wife than by the husband. When obtained on her
petition, she took away with her all the property she
had brought her husband, all her husband had settled
upon her on their marriage, and in addition so much
of her husband's property as her industry appeared
to have entitled her to. This latter would be little
or nothing if she had been an idle woman, a considerable amount if she had been a good housewife
and producer of wealth. It was estimated in various
ways according to circumstances. Supposing there
was a quantity of flax or wool on the premises, if this
remained in the raw state until the woman obtained

her divorce she could take away none of it unless
she was able to establish a claim in some other way,
which she might do up to the value of one-eighth of
the raw material. If by her industry she had it " in
locks," she was entitled to take away one sixth of it;
if combed, one-third; and so on; the assumption
being that she had made these improvements. In
making these calculations various matters of set-off
arose with which we need not trouble ourselves here.
The law seems to contemplate a woman being
divorced from her husband and marrying him again,
and even doing this more than once. Possibly
divorce is a redundant translation, that the marriage
was not considered completely dissolved, and that
separation would be more nearly correct.

According to these laws a man might purchase a
wife; from which it would follow that what a man
might buy he might also sell. The English laws of
Æthelbirht and of Ine distinctly provide for the
buying of a wife. The Irish laws have much more
to say about the abduction than about the purchase
of wives. The laws recognised three relations
between men and women. In the first of these
stood " a first lawful wife; " in the second " a first
lawful adaltrach-woman; " in the third " an adaltrach-woman of abduction." All were legal relations,
and could not be dissolved except by the will of both
parties or by legal process. These relations are not
defined; but I believe that the first was the only
one that had a religious sanction, and that the
second and third were merely civil relations, the

third being distinctly stuprous and of itself scarcely
conferring any right.

Apparently the law on marriage and the dissolution of marriage was wholly pagan, and never
underwent any modification in Christian times;
perhaps because it was little resorted to except by
the wealthy, and they had sufficient influence to keep
it unaltered.   Besides, it is impossible to know how
we may err in attempting to apply laws to a form of
society which we do not understand.   I am con-
vinced that the law on this subject must not be
taken as presenting a true picture of ancient Irish
life, not because the picture is an unfavourable one,
but because outside the laws there is overwhelming
evidence that this legal picture is unjust, that
singular purity characterised the Irish in the past as
in the present, and that women occupied in ancient
times a position as honourable as they occupy now.
It is one of the many cases in which the law is more
concerned with the few who invoke it than with the
many who never invoke it during their lives.
Probably all the value that should be attached to
the law on this subject is that it marks the extreme
limit of libertinism.

SECTION II.

FOSTERAGE.

OSTERAGE was such an important feature of Irish social life that, although only a custom, elaborate rules relating to it were laid down in the laws; and we cannot omit noticing the subject, however briefly.

Fosterage was the custom of placing children during their minority in charge of other members of the clan. It was usually restricted to members of the *fine*, which has been described and which chiefly consisted of persons within the fifth degree of kindred; but there was no strict rule on this point. It was practised by all classes, but especially by the wealthy, by chiefs and leading men. It is not clear what, besides the force of habit, was the motive for it; but its practice, whether designed for that end or not, helped materially to strengthen the natural ties of kinship and sympathy which bound the chief and clan or the flaith and sept together. Quite apart from law, the relations arising from fosterage were in popular estimation the most sacred of the whole social system, and a stronger affection oftentimes sprang up between persons standing in those relations than that between immediate relatives by birth.

There were various kinds of fosterage, and minute rules are laid down for all, especially with reference to the mode of treating the children in fosterage according to the position they were intended to fill in after life, the amount payable by the different classes for the different kinds of fosterage, the relations between the child and its foster parents both during the fosterage and after, and various other matters. Foster parents were bound under heavy penalties to teach their foster children or have them taught, whether boys or girls, the branches of knowledge, business, trades, or exercises suited to their rank. During the fosterage the foster father was liable for injuries and offences committed by the foster child, and entitled to compensation for any injury done to the foster child.

A peculiar variety, called literary fosterage, was practised by ollamhs. Ollamhs taught pupils of the ordinary sort in the ordinary way, for payment or for nothing according to circumstances; but they also took a limited number of pupils into a particular kind of fosterage combined with pupilage, adopted them into their families, and so thoroughly imbued them with the spirit of the profession they were about to enter that the original family ties of those pupils became as if they had never existed.

As a rule a child was not sent to fosterage until it was one year old. " There are three periods at which fosterage ends : death, crime, and selection." Selection meant marriage; and the legal age of selection was reached by girls at the end of fourteen years, and by boys at the end of seventeen years. Foster parents who had properly discharged their duties were entitled in old age to be supported by their foster children, if they were in need and had no children of their own.

The law of fosterage seems to search out, ransack, and provide for every domestic possibility. It is perfectly amazing to find so many rules relating to domestic economy, and to contrast the modern absence of rule on such matters. Let me give an illustration. Expounding the cāin law of fosterage some worthy ollamh writes in this fashion—" What are their victuals ? *Leite*=stirabout is given to them all ; but the flavouring (literally *dip*) which goes into it is different ; namely, salt butter for the sons of the inferior grades, fresh butter for the sons of chieftains, honey for the sons of kings. The food of each continues the same respectively until the end of one year, or three years [according to the kind of fosterage]. Stirabout made of oatmeal on butter-milk or water is given to the sóns of the Feini grades, and a bare sufficiency of it merely, and salt butter for flavouring. Stirabout made on new milk is given to the sons of the chieftain grades, and fresh butter for flavouring, and a full sufficiency of it is given to them; and this stirabout is made of barley-meal. Stirabout made on new milk is given to the sons of kings, and it is made of wheaten meal, and honey for flavouring." This passage will convey an idea of the small matters of which the law took cognizance. Skene, the author of *Celtic Scotland*, says that the word "stirabout" is unknown out of Ireland, and quoting this passage he substitutes the word "porridge."

SECTION III.

CONTRACTS AND WILLS.

ONTRACTS between individuals do not assume great importance among a people organised in clans until clan responsibility has begun to give place to the responsibility of individuals. The provisions of the clan system, coupled with the simple country life of our ancestors, left little occasion for contracts either of the commercial sort or under seal among them; and the same system so fully provided for the devolution of their property after their death that there was hardly any occasion for wills. In transferring property in goods, barter, which was far more extensively employed than true sale, was in general more conclusive and gave rise to fewer questions for legal decision. Contracts relating to land were not numerous. They could in general be made only with the concurrence of the sept and in the presence of a flaith of high rank called the *Aire-forgaill.* Some written contracts relating to land have been preserved, perhaps from the fourteenth century; but while other writings of apparently less private importance are carefully dated, these are without date. It is at first sight strange that written contracts and wills were so little used among a people so addicted to writing on other subjects. The explanation is, that the clan system rendered them unnecessary. They were exceptional and foreign to that system, and while it continued in effective operation the amount of property affected by contracts and wills was probably not great. Nevertheless, some rules relating to wills are laid down in the *Corus Bescna;* and the Senchus Mōr contains a good deal about contracts, from which it is clear that warranty on the sale of goods was well understood and frequently given and taken; and the importance of a valuable consideration, not generally recognised in English law until the last century, was perfectly well known in Ireland. Anything done without valuable consideration is described as done "for God's sake," and imposed a very slight if any legal obligation on the other party to it. From the expression frequently used that "Nothing is due without deserving it," we must infer that a valuable consideration was essential to the binding of a contract of any kind.

It also appears that to form a contract perfect and legally binding a witness was necessary, that this witness should in general be of the tribe of the party on whom the performance of the contract lay, that his status was an important legal element, and that by acting as witness he incurred the liabilities of a surety.

Many rules are given as to the times within which in different circumstances sales might be set aside. A contract of two sane adults, with knowledge and warranty, might, on fraud being discovered, be dissolved in twenty-four hours. Without knowledge and without warranty it might be dissolved for ten days after the fraud was discovered. In both cases the "knowledge" is that of the buyer. The law seems more concerned about the state of the buyer's mind at the time of the purchase than about that of the seller.

Ratification of contracts made by persons under subjection and therefore not fully entitled to contract was also well understood. "One is held to adopt what he does not repudiate after knowledge, having power."

From a passage I have quoted it would appear that, as in English law until recently, a married woman was merged in her husband while he lived, and could not be bound by any contract made by her. This, however, is subject to some qualification, for it is clear from other passages that a woman could contract, in the presence of her husband, to the amount of her own honour-price.

Few married women had either taste or occasion for asserting what are now called women's rights.

A boy was deemed to have no sense until he was seven years old, only half sense from seven to the end of his fifteenth year. Even after this period he had strictly no power to contract so long as he remained a member of his father's household; but if he did make a contract with his father's knowledge it was binding on the father unless promptly repudiated. If once ratified by the father it was treated as his contract.

Monks on becoming such lost the capacity of contracting; but a monk who became abbot, or was appointed to manage the temporal affairs of his community, was allowed to contract on behalf of the community.

The non-free had very meagre powers of contracting, and the lowest grade of them had none at all.

SECTION IV.

ARTISANS.

 NE does not expect to find much in these ancient laws relating specially to artisans. The ordinary law applied to them as to other people, and they were not sufficiently numerous to call for special treatment. We are told that their social status was determined by the rank of those for whom they worked. If this was so, its effect in practice probably was to make the position of artisan to a chief an object of ambition in each particular craft and the reward of superior skill in that craft; and if the artisan continued to progress, his status would rise *pari passu* with his skill—a very just arrangement. Workers in gold and others who practised what might be called fine arts, the results of which were required only by the

wealthy, must under the same arrangement have stood high in the social scale. Smiths, too, were always held in high esteem. Some of the more important artisans were supplied with free lands for their support; others were paid wages, which appear to have been fixed, in theory at least, by the law. We have already noticed the power of artisans to form guilds or partnerships in virtue of which they could acquire political and social rights; and we have also noticed some liabilities connected with their trades, in the chapter on crime.

It was customary with artificers, on completing a work and delivering it to the employer, to pronounce a blessing on it. So strong was the feeling on this subject, that a workman who refused to give the blessing was fined. It would seem that the first who saw a work newly finished by another was also expected to bless the work. This was extreme sensibility; but as the blessing was general the shock caused by its omission was great. When I first came to London I was shocked on meeting persons asking alms without adding the words, "for God's sake," and taking alms without uttering a prayer in return; for neither is ever omitted in Ireland.

SECTION V.

OATHS.

HERE does not appear to have been at any time in ancient Ireland one fixed form of oath or manner of swearing in legal proceedings. The Brehon Laws do not tell us much of how our pagan fathers swore. There is no doubt at all that they did swear; and, if writings not of a legal character are to be trusted, they swore on solemn occasions by the sun, moon, wind, and other elements, the dew, the crops, and the countenances of men. Ugaine Mōr, before his death in A.M. 4606, "exacted oaths, by all the elements visible and invisible, from the men of Erinn in general that they would never contend for the sovereignty of Erinn with his children or his race" (*Four Masters*). In Christian times a similar variety of oaths prevailed, all differing in legal value. The oath of highest value was that taken on the Gospels; but an oath taken on a relic, on a shrine or reliquary, or on a bishop's crosier, was also deemed very solemn and binding. Again, the value of the oath differed according to the place in which it was taken. Sometimes it was taken in the house of the person swearing, sometimes at the grave of those dearest to him, sometimes in a court of justice, sometimes in a church before the altar. That at the grave was probably of pagan origin. In some cases the oath was not a simple oath, but a triple one; the person swore first standing, then sitting, and then lying, as he spent his life.

"The king excells all in testimony, for he can, by his mere word, decide against every class of persons, except those of the two orders of religion and learning who are of equal rank with him." This is still generally so in monarchies.

CHAPTER IX.

NATIVE, NOT ROMAN.

T is said in the State Papers by an English official in Ireland in Queen Elizabeth's reign that, " this Feinechas is none other than the sivill law ; " and the saying is occasionally repeated even to the present time. That the statement is, however, none other than incorrect, might easily be shown by going through both the Civil Law and the Irish law seriatim. The present little treatise, without being at all designed for that purpose, will render this sufficiently obvious. There are no two systems of law of which I have any knowledge which do not contain some points in common. It would be strange indeed if men devising rules for the extensive field of human conduct, and for determining all sorts of rights and obligations, did not happen to hit upon the same expedient occasionally. Their doing

so proves their common humanity. To prove the
alleged derivation much more is required. But the
fact is, that in the Brehon Laws such coincidences
with Roman Law are really fewer than might be
expected without derivation at all. The coincidences
with Hindoo Law are actually more numerous; yet
no one suggests that the Brehon Laws are derived
from the Hindoo.

Some rules of church law, itself based on the later
Roman Law, were introduced obviously by the
Christian clergy, and affected mainly themselves
and their interests. They are fewer and less important than might have been expected, owing to
the Celtic organisation which the Church early
assumed, and for many centuries retained. There
is also the supposed resemblance which the collection of laws called the Senchus Mōr bears to the
Roman collections called the Digest and the Pan-
dects. To press this as a proof of derivation would
be absurd, for there is really no more in it than in
the resemblance in distant perspective between two
trees in a forest. The laws were collected as they
existed; and if when collected they happened to
resemble some other collection, there was nothing
to wonder at, the laws could not help it, and it does
not prove their derivation from that other. Analogies
are very tempting, but often misleading; and such a
superficial analogy as this would be a very unsafe
guide. If the Brehon Laws had been at all derived
from Roman Law, the resemblances would have been
far more numerous, intimate, and vital, the whole

juridical structure would probably have been different, and with the law itself some of the Roman technical terms would have been adopted, as in all countries that have really copied from Roman Law. None of those terms are found in the Irish manuscripts. Many of the Irish laws are as old as the Roman Law itself. Whether they are good or bad, creditable or otherwise to our race, they are essentially, substantially, and characteristically Irish. Sir Samuel Ferguson expressed the literal truth when he wrote that "The Roman (or Civil) Law is hardly traceable in them, except as regards ecclesiastical affairs, and that *sub modo* only."

Without desiring to suggest whether they would or would not have been better if they had been derived from Roman Law, it may be interesting to point out that the Irish laws were in several respects more humane than the Roman. The Irish *flaith-fine* never at any time had power of life and death over the members of his household, as the Roman paterfamilias unquestionably had in early times. Then with regard to the treatment of strangers : at Rome, for a long time, an alien was an enemy, who might be ill used, whose property was *res nullius* which any Roman might seize, and who had no *locus standi* whatever before a legal tribunal. In Ireland a stranger was a person entitled to sympathy, his property could not be taken from him, and not alone was he heard in a court of law, but he was allowed to choose his judge. "Whenever a person comes over the sea to prosecute a cause, he shall have a

choice of the Brehons of Erinn ; and when he shall
have come across the boundary of a province, he
shall have his choice of the brehons in the province." We have already seen that unjust evasion
of a stranger was punished as fraud.

There was much resemblance between the Irish
laws and those of ancient Britain, so far as the
latter can be discerned through the native Welsh
laws, between which and the Irish there is a good
deal in common. All British laws were modified
under Roman sway, which Ireland escaped. Of
course the laws of the Gaels of Scotland were
originally our laws transferred to Scotland. They,
however, underwent considerable change, for feudalism was vigorously forced upon Scotland in the
Middle Ages.

CHAPTER X.

CONCLUSION.

(Hibernice : The Conclusion Begins Down Here.)

HE Danes were the first wreckers of purely **Gaelic** institutions in Ireland. Though their power was broken at Clontarf, so also, in the death of Brian and his son, was destroyed the rising hope of an immediate and thoroughly national restoration of Celtic institutions and forms which had been interrupted. The interruption becoming permanent, the spell of attachment was broken, and some of those institutions and forms became definitely extinct. Instead of a speedy return of vigorous national life, there was a state of doubtful oscillation between relapse and convalescence. Recovery was not complete when the

Anglo-Normans came and put an eternal period to
its progress. The Celtic system was indeed maintained over the greater part of the country; but
only in its shattered and incomplete condition, and
only with a view to the interests of isolated and
rival communities or rival individuals; never
universally or with a view to the interests of the
nation as a whole, and never with the old unques-
tioned power and full reverential obedience. The
Anglo-Irish, wherever they were sprinkled throughout the country, except the Pale, did in the main
adopt Irish laws, language, dress, and customs; and
such of them as attained sufficient power became
Irish chiefs, and appointed their own brehons in the
Irish way. But the nation considered as a political
unit had lost the essential organism and attributes
of a state, and the statesmanship of England was
directed to the prevention of re-organisation and the
fomenting of disorder. In obedience to this statesmanship a so-called parliament, consisting mainly of
self-elected English officials, was held in Kilkenny
in 1367, and an Act was passed, written not in Irish,
nor even in English, but in Norman-French, brand-
ing the Irish as enemies, and penalising the adoption
of their dress, manners, language, and laws.
Various other measures conceived in a like spirit
followed. They were not immediately successful in
their direct object; but they were too successful in
sowing discord among people who wanted only to be
let alone, and they armed and created an opportunity
for miscreant adventurers hungry for a morsel of

prey. This latter was the main object of those measures. The trade of fomenting disorder throve apace. It was the only trade that did. The Gaelic race, with its peculiar institutions, national and domestic, was kept disorganised until disorganisation became its normal condition. It was not so much that civilisation was undergoing a change as that it was being strangled. There were two nations in the land, animated not by a desire to evolve a better condition of things, but by a mutual desire to thwart each other at every hand's turn. Neither was able to establish a central government of its own of sufficient potency to enforce its own views. Each was able and willing to prevent the other from doing it. It is doubtful that either correctly understood the true remedy of the evil they jointly created; and certain that they would not have adopted the true remedy if they had understood it. All over the country, except the Pale, the Brehon Laws, like sun through storm, prevailed in some way; for other law there was none.

The so-called parliaments held before the reign of Henry the Eighth were organised mainly by hungry adventurers and in their interest, and consisted of themselves, their friends and connections in office, and knights of the Pale. Hardly any Gaelic Irishmen attended them, and many were unaware of their existence. During the reigns of Henry the Eighth, Edward the Sixth, and Mary, a semblance of English institutions gradually grew upon the country, not by reason of their superiority, but

partly with the hope that their adoption would, as a
concession to English prejudice, contribute somewhat to peace, and partly owing to the enforced
decay of all that was native.   I need not tell how,
in Elizabeth's bloody reign, the hope was blasted,
the work of destruction carried on by fire and sword,
craft and poison, and Teutonic institutions set up on
the ruins.   The great transformation was completed
under James the First, and confirmed and rendered
irrevocable under Charles the First, Cromwell, and
William the Third.   Such old brehons and ollamhs
as may have been then living sank into obscurity
and into the grave without successors.   Night had
fallen on the Gael, and Justice as a living presence
had been banished from among them.

   In the third, fourth, and probably all future
volumes of the Brehon Laws the student will find
elaborate introductions written by the editors, no
doubt in good faith, for his guidance.   From the
same volumes he will miss the simpler and safer
Gaelic guidance of O'Donovan and O'Curry.   He
will soon realise that he has passed into the hands
of men of Teutonic instinct, training, and sympathies,
and under alien, if not unfriendly guidance.   Should
he be so much in earnest about his subject that his
guides do not succeed in disgusting him with it, as
they are apt to do, he will begin to realise that it
would have been just as well for his progress and for
their reputation if those elaborate introductions had
never been written.   When he has begun to relish
and digest the Brehon Laws in spite of the introduc-

tions, his success in acquiring a knowledge of them is assured, and the rate of his further progress will correspond with the rate at which he frees himself from their guidance.

As a classic poet may be translated in such a way as to make him look ridiculous, so it is conceivable that of two presentations of these laws equally true in substance one may be positively unfair. Without being intentionally unfair, those introductions are distinctly so in effect. Originating in a Teutonic mind, they are based on the initial assumption that the Teuton alone of all mankind is capable of devising and attaining perfection in legal and political institutions, and that the Irish Celt is incapable of either devising them or adopting them when devised by others. The notion is so grotesque as not to be worth contradicting. But why has its expression been given a place in our national documents? It is clearly the offspring of mental bias, however acquired or however unconscious. The sum paid to this un-Irish editor was, I fear, too small; yet it was probably quite as much as his Irish predecessors had been paid, and so long as he did take it one cannot help thinking that he might have been a little more polite towards a nation good enough to pay it.

Of many passages in which the Teutonic type is set up as the standard of perfection and anything differing from it stamped as barbarous, one sentence taken at random will be quite enough as a specimen. "An act is criminal in the correct use of the word when it is regarded as an offence against the State."

Observe the word "correct." What does it mean here? It means "English." Or, expanded, it means "In accordance with the present English theory of crime, in which I have been instructed." The editor seems quite oblivious of the fact that if he had been instructed in a different system his "correct" would have a different meaning, that if he had been instructed solely in English law of a past age his "correct" would have a different meaning. Which of these meanings, then, would be truly correct? I think none of them. In such matters there is no such thing as perfect abstract correctness universal and eternal. The most correct in one set of circumstances might be the most incorrect in another. To set up any one system, however good, as the only correct system for all mankind in all ages, is not alone incorrect, but is absurd arrogance. Our ancestors happened to think, as some of ourselves think, that a wrongful act, knowingly and wilfully committed against another person, contained in itself all the essentials of a crime, irrespective of the manner in which the State regarded it. Of course this alien editor would object that this is confounding the moral view with the legal, a thing abhorrent to an English lawyer. A brehon would ask in astonishment, What harm if they are confounded? If the moral view is enforced by law it becomes the legal view as well, and there is harmony instead of unnatural antagonism.

An exponent of Gaelic law who can, without seeing the impropriety, write of *English* law as "our ancient law," as Mr. Richey does, appears to me to stand self-condemned. It is a confession, if it be not a boast, that he must not be regarded as a native exponent. Deliberately taking up the position, not of a friendly editor, but of a foreign and more or less adverse critic, he scrutinises his subject from aloft or from without. To him these are at best ancient laws, and at that only Irish ancient laws. To us they are much more. They are OUR ANCIENT LAWS emphatically. Nations, like individuals, have their heirlooms, which they do not like to see disrespectfully used. If a Scotch advocate were stupid enough to commit in a treatise on Scotch law such a blunder as that just pointed out he would be completely discredited. It is only for Irish laws this treatment is considered good enough.

The matters in which the foreign mind of the editor manifests itself are mostly small, taken singly, but scattered over a volume or two, positively in statements and negatively in omissions, they produce a lasting effect. Even defect of knowledge which hundreds of living Irish men and women could have supplied is to be met with; as where a note of interrogation is inserted after the word *dilesc*, a form of *duileasg*, the name of a sea-plant well known under both its English and its Irish names all round the coast, and to be seen on the stalls of market women. The editor apparently did not condescend to ask information from such people.

To acquire perfect knowledge of a difficult subject, as to acquire skill in a difficult art, one needs the inspiration and guidance of some degree of affection, or at least tolerant sympathy. Unless he takes the ideas to himself, and warms them in his own breast, they are like stricken roses which never open, and he inevitably misses or misunderstands some portion of them. To be able to present in the English language a true picture of the Gaelic laws, one requires much more than philological knowledge, literary skill, and a keen legal perception. He obviously requires to imbibe the Gaelic spirit to some extent if it is not naturally his. Why not? Otherwise "it is the lark and not the nightingale." He requires a heart attuned to the Gaelic pulse, a mind capable of understanding, for the time at least, the Gaelic mode of reasoning: and this necessity is rendered not less imperative but more so by the fact that the Gaelic pulse now beats low and has done so for some time past. It does beat still, and may even yet beat strongly once more; for it is the native pulse of many who now know it not. Still "There is many a man of the race of Conn in beautiful Erinn of the smooth grass," and many more elsewhere. No one can expound those laws unless he understands them, and to understand them one must treat them respectfully, somewhat as one would treat flowers he had found preserved amongst the leaves of a deceased friend's book, or the cerements of a mummy. They will not yield their sweetness to him if he tosses them disdainfully as with a pitch-fork. It is a privilege to be allowed to meddle with them, and ought not to be done as though it were an irksome task grudgingly performed. The editor of whom I complain has not squandered any affection on these laws. What one does not respect he does not warm in his bosom. One does not imbibe a spirit he despises.

I am quite aware that opinions such as mine have to contend, and often to contend in vain, against the universal disposition, unusually developed in the Teutonic temperament, to spurn the suggestion that any people have peculiarities which outsiders cannot understand as well as themselves. This disposition is fortified by the acknowledged importance of seeing ourselves as others see us. The vision of others may be true, while our own may be partial. The opinions of an unfriendly critic may be sound, so far as he understands the subject. My contention is, that the principle of seeing ourselves as others see us may be carried too far on one side, that so far as it is good it is universally applicable, that Teutonic peoples do not pay us for telling how we see them, that there is much in human life and manners which outsiders never can by any means perceive, and not perceiving never can understand or describe, and that the translation of our own laws at our own expense was an occasion when the Gaelic view was unquestionably the view that ought to have been presented above all others.

No one presumes to claim that either the laws or the brehons were perfect. They would indeed have been wonderful, and out of place in this world, had they been perfect. It is very easy to point out imperfections in both. The laws were in many respects painfully restrictive, in many crude and seriously defective according to our conceptions. But why should we expect the Brehon Laws, any more than other *leges barbarorum* with which they may be classed, to suit modern conceptions or to be adaptable to the complex texture of the modern world ? They were never intended for that. If they suited ancient conceptions they fulfilled the object of their institution. That they did this to as large an extent as any other laws, past or present, is sufficiently established by the enormous length of time during which they continued in force, and in force, remember, by the will of the people. In considering them it should be borne in mind throughout, but especially when any startling feature is met with, that it is not with modern laws they ought to be compared, but with those of their own time. This test they bear well, so far as it can be applied ; and from such a comparison we have no occasion to shrink. But the fact is that few modern nations possess material sufficiently old for instituting this comparison, and what they do possess of ancient date is mainly concerned with crimes. To be sure, the Irish laws ought to have been gradually adapted to the changed conditions of the people. But then they would have lost in the process that archaic character in which their chief interest now lies. Even now, tried by our modern consciences and searched by our modern lights, they afford sufficient evidence that all perfection is not modern. Side by side with the crude, and equally archaic with it, are some principles which modern legislators might adopt with advantage. The desire just now so prevalent to found courts of arbitration and conciliation is the best practical tribute that could be paid to the wisdom of our ancestors, as shown in the consensual character of the brehon's jurisdiction. Every competent and impartial reader of these laws will admit that their merits far outnumber their defects, that they were animated by a spirit of justice and a desire to secure fair dealing, especially to those who needed that security, and that they were highly creditable as an attempt to harmonise conflicting rights. These must always be important objects of law; and that they should be attained in each age and country in its own way is the important thing, not the manner of their attainment. The development of legal ideas was not uniform in Ireland. It never has been uniform anywhere.

The remarkably just character of the Brehon Laws has been attributed to the fact that for centuries they were not meddled with by rulers or ruled, but were moulded to a large extent by the brehons, who occupied a neutral position. This, if it be correct, adds to the merit of the brehons when the reader is reminded that throughout the whole range of English law what is judge-made can nearly always be traced by its execrable character.

In almost every respect the Brehon Laws bear comparison very well with English laws not so old. English laws from the time of Alfred, and perhaps

17

before it, down to the present day, have been constantly disfigured by hardships and disabilities imposed upon people on account of their religion or their want of religion, and by ghastly, absurd, and generally vain efforts to force people's consciences. *Of course* there is not a trace of these absurdities to be found in the Irish laws. Our ancestors, like ourselves, had faith in reason and good example, not in the thumbscrew. They thought that penal laws ought to be applied only to criminal acts, and that the consciences of harmless people ought to be let alone.

The odious system of torture called the *ordeal,* so common in the Middle Ages, by which evidence was roasted or boiled, according to taste, out of unwilling witnesses, and confessions of guilt wrung often from persons perfectly innocent ; this was never known in Ireland, except possibly in the Pale. There is not a word about it in the Brehon Laws. Englishmen, never short of an excuse when their own national reputation is concerned, have no better to offer for the practice of the ordeal than that it was universal. Even this poor excuse, however, is not valid ; for, small though Ireland is, a thing never practised there was not universal.

Now with more direct regard to the brehons and ollamhs, any modern reader will be at once struck with the want of scientific arrangement in their work, and with the manner in which they open a new subject, in the middle, so to speak, instead of at the beginning as we should desire. Language apparently simple is found to be most difficult and disappointing for want of the primary foundations and proper definitions. Initial facts and principles are assumed, not explained. We constantly feel that only a part of the law is revealed to us, the writer assuming that we know the rest. Nowhere is an attempt made to grapple with any branch of law and give a complete exposition of it throughout. It is easy to point out defects like these, because they lie on the surface, and are the first a reader encounters. They are serious obstacles, and may disgust him ; but they do not affect the law itself. They are but its shell, a rough shell, which must be cracked before the kernel can be reached. To murmur against the brehons for these defects would be about as reasonable as to murmur against them for not having delivered judgments into phonographs. This is the nineteenth century, not the tenth. The brehons did not live in a scientific age. Are not the very defects of their work interesting, if not instructive, to us ? Should our little difficulties prevent our appreciating the enormous difficulties they had to surmount ? Though most of the matter we have been considering was written more than a thousand years ago, much of it is marked by a clearness of expression which modern Acts of Parliament do not always attain. The connection of the brehons and ollamhs with the law was too long and intimate to allow of our entirely withholding either praise or blame from them as the laws may seem to merit. But before blaming we should be very sure that we understand. We should remember that with our best efforts we can never acquire more than a partial knowledge of these men and their laws. We can never successfully free ourselves from our own surroundings, and cast ourselves back into their world, or revive its conditions around ourselves. The brehons and ollamhs knew, far better than we can ever realise, what an inadequate picture of themselves and their laws these writings would present if a time should come when no other picture remained, nor living voice to tell the mysteries of this, wherein it is full, wherein it wholly fails. That time has come, and to it and our imperfect vision much that is distorted or unintelligible may very justly be attributed.

The student of legal history, Roman and English, will turn from exasperating auspices and fantastic ceremonial, and all the cruel delay and injustice of which these were the guilty occasion, and will give credit to the brehons for their manly good sense in not inventing artificial meshes for their own feet and the feet of those who sought justice at their hands. That a man had moral right on his side did not matter a pin's point to the old-fashioned judges of Rome and of London if their fantastic technicalities had not been complied with. In no instance in the Brehon Laws have I met with an outrage upon justice for the sake of mere form, a thing quite common under the Formal system at Rome, quite common in England until a few years ago, and possible even now, as in the case of *Kendall versus Hamilton*.

The brehons of the Gaelic decadence, owing mainly to political causes, have left us little whereby to gauge their capacity. For this it would ill become us to blame them. It is a mistake to suppose that to transmit judgments to posterity to criticise is at any time the highest duty of a judge. If in the disorder of their times they managed still to make just laws prevail amongst their contemporaries against the law of the strong hand, they performed their whole duty, and a difficult one it must have been. Through no fault of theirs their rulings, once executing themselves *proprio vigore*, were no longer universally obeyed. Their sphere of influence was shrinking, and with it virility of thought. We, however, cannot be indifferent to the fact that if they had neither the ability nor the opportunity to add to or develop the laws, they had at least the judgment and grace to preserve them. It is easy to be wise after events, and to point out in what respects things might have been better had they been managed differently. It is easy, but not brave, to censure those who cannot return to explain. Not even the wise men of the nineteenth century can penetrate far into the future, nor do they always understand the hidden springs of their own conduct or the drift of their own acts; and in their most pretentious efforts they may be merely spoiling some possibilities of the future. Since the days of the brehons man's powers and purposes have increased and multiplied tenfold. We shall not be deemed unworthy members of society if, with our enlarged facilities, we deserve as well of our own age as the brehons did of theirs.

Law at best is not the most fascinating of subjects. Very handsome things have been said of it, and justly; but they have been said mostly by lawyers. It is, among other things, the bulwark of the righteous, the shield of the weak, the noble science of discovering in circumstances of great complexity what is just, and making the [balance play on its pivot with strict impartiality. It may also be considered as a very vulgar business, mainly connected with, and sometimes debased to the promotion of, what is sordid and criminal. Whichever view be taken, the importance of the law of a country cannot ;be disputed. There are many important things connected with ancient Ireland yet to be learned; few more so than that which we have been considering. A nation's law is an irrebuttable witness to its character, a mirror that cannot be disclaimed. We should in justice remember that it is in general an unfavourable witness, an unflattering mirror. It reflects cases, disputes, quarrels, and lends undue importance to the comparatively few members of the population who figure in them, while almost wholly ignoring all the sweetness and goodness of human life and the vast numbers who pass through life without a legal dispute at all. It takes little notice of duties faithfully discharged, but is endlessly garrulous about obligations broken. It provides against offences which are rarely committed, and disregards the good acts with which the hours are studded. In a vast flock, which it apparently sees not, it spies with eagle eye the distempered kid. It is so little concerned with quiet folk who all their lives do right and justice that if left to legal reading one might suppose they did not exist; so much concerned with wrong and wrong-doers that if left to legal reading one might judge the world very uncharitably indeed. These remarks in the abstract apply neither more nor less to Irish than to other laws. But in the case of other laws that are now read, the effect on the reader's mind is usually counteracted by other miscellaneous literature of the nation to which the laws belong, while it is likely that many who will read this little treatise on Irish laws will not be fortified with much miscellaneous reading in reference to ancient Ireland. Persons for whom the quiet voices of ancient peace and harmony are wholly still, and to whom the best types of our race are wholly unknown, will here make acquaintance with ancient disputes and with the aspects of men in contest. These, unrelieved, will linger in the memory, and these alone the mention of ancient Ireland will recall. In truth, they formed little of the real ancient Ireland, and I now feel guilty of having in some measure contributed to their posthumous importance.

Having read some of those ancient laws, and made some notes as I proceeded, the thought occurred to me that, although the subject is dry and harsh as all laws are, and although it is stale and obsolete which other laws are not, still there might be some who would take sufficient interest in the subject to read my notes if reduced to order. On comparing the notes and setting them together, as so many fragments of a broken vessel, I found that considerably more than half of them were utterly useless for my purpose, belonging apparently to vessels of which I had no conception, and quite irreconcilable as parts of one structure. All the fragments were doubtless genuine, if one only knew their respective times and districts. In the vast expanse of time over which those laws extend many varieties of law and practice must necessarily have arisen from local, temporary, and accidental causes. To follow all these and treat them adequately would demand several volumes. Hence many fragments, in themselves interesting, had to be sacrificed, and some whole branches of substantive law, as the law of taking possession of land, and the very important law of suretiship, had to be either wholly admitted or compressed into a few obscure sentences of a sub-section. The rest I do not pretend to have treated as they deserve to be treated by an Irishman and a lawyer ; and though availing of the assistance of those who have gone before me, even of some with whose views I herein expressly disagree, I may possibly have gone astray myself on some points. Other writers retaining fragments which I reject, may, with perfect fidelity to truth, have educed, or may yet educe, legal structures and conceptions of Brehon Law inconsistent with mine. I claim no more than to present the laws as I understand them, well aware that even in my own conception of them there are points difficult to reconcile and explain. I am also quite aware of my silence on several legal matters on which information is very desirable. The laws themselves are silent on these matters, and the importance we attach to them may be due to our own surroundings. If any one should open this little book with great expectations he will close it with disappointment correspondingly great. I have neither treated the whole subject descriptively, nor entered into an exhaustive criticism of any part of it. To do either satisfactorily within this compass were quite impossible. It is not every man can put a gallon of liquid into a pint bottle. My aim is to interest the general reader, to put within the reach of all who desire some knowledge of those laws a convenient synopsis of their leading features, with some corrections of current errors, and above all to induce some student better equipped than I to undertake a thorough examination of those laws and treat the world to a work really worthy of the subject and calculated to take the wind completely out of my small sail. To succeed in any one of these respects would be not to have worked in vain ; success in the last mentioned is the summit of my ambition.

END.

18

CPSIA information can be obtained
at www.ICGtesting.com
Printed in the USA
BVOW03s1137131017
497589BV00001B/11/P